Archives in Pennsylvania for Genealogy Research

A Guide to Records in Colleges, Courthouses, Genealogical Societies, Historic Sites, Historical Societies, Libraries, and Museums

Denyse Allen

PA Ancestors L.L.C.

Copyright © 2024 by Denyse Allen and PA Ancestors L.L.C.

All rights reserved.

No portion of this book may be reproduced in any form without written permission from the publisher or author, except as permitted by U.S. copyright law.

This publication is designed to provide accurate and authoritative information in regard to the subject matter covered. It is sold with the understanding that neither the author nor the publisher is engaged in rendering legal, Investment, accounting or other professional services. While the publisher and author have used their best efforts in preparing this book, they make no representations or warranties with respect to the accuracy or completeness of the contents of this book and specifically disclaim any implied warranties of merchantability or fitness for a particular purpose. The advice and strategies contained herein may not be suitable for your situation. You should consult with a professional when appropriate. Neither the publisher nor the author shall be liable for any loss of profit or any other commercial damages, including but not limited to special, incidental, consequential, personal, or other damages.

Book Cover by Denyse Allen

Images on front cover all taken by author. Locations, from top right, going clockwise: The Pennsylvania State Archive entrance, 350 North Street, Harrisburg; Historical Society of Pennsylvania, Philadelphia; Conshohocken Historical Society, Conshohocken; Carnegie Library, Forbes Avenue, Pittsburgh; Philadelphia City Archives, Philadelphia; Centre County Library and Historical Museum, Bellefonte; Northeast Pennsylvania Genealogical Society, Wilkes-Barre; Penn State Pattee Library, University Park.

*To my ancestors John Wilmer and Robinson Curry
who eluded me in the usual records*

Contents

Introduction 1

1. What You Can Find in Archives 7
   Family Letters
   Iron Furnace Time Books
   Store Keeper Ledgers
   Institutional Records

2. Creating Your Plan for Archival Research 17
   How Archives Came to Be
   Why You Need a Research Question
   Crafting Your Research Question
   Researching Events, Organizations, and Locations

3. Using Catalogs and Finding Aids 23
   How Archives are Organized
   Types of Archive Catalogs
   Archival Finding Aids
   Shifting Your Mindset
   Create the Research Profile

4. Researching in Archives in Person or From Home 35
   Research Trips in Person
   Research Requests Through Mail (or Email)
   Hiring a Researcher

5. State-Wide Archives 47
   Pennsylvania State Archives
   State Library of Pennsylvania
   Historical Society of Pennsylvania

Genealogical Society of Pennsylvania

National Archives and Record Administration, Philadelphia Branch

FamilySearch Affiliate Libraries and FamilySearch Centers

6. Regional Pennsylvania Archives — 69

Penn State University, Eberly Family Special Collections Library

Heinz History Center, Detre Library and Archives

Temple University Libraries, Special Collections Research Center

Philadelphia Area Consortium of Special Collections Libraries (PACSCL)

7. County Courthouses and Archives — 83

County Offices and Duties

How to Start Researching in County Records

County Records Available Online

8. Archives and Special Collections at Colleges and Universities — 113

9. Local Organizational, Historical, and Genealogical Archives — 131

10. Federal and State Historical Sites — 195

11. Religious Organization Archives — 201

12. Wrapping Up and Saving Your Research — 221

Take Digital Images

Beware of Copyright

Organize and Back-Up

A Few Final Thoughts

Terms Used by Archives — 225

Sources — 229

About the Author — 231

Bonus Materials — 233

Introduction

How would it feel to hold a paper from 100 years ago with your ancestor's name on it?

What about a document they signed in 1750? Or perhaps a photograph from 1910 that you never knew existed?

All of this is possible when you research in archives.

For most of us our daily attention is filled with digital images on screens – phone screens, computer screens and television screens.

Meanwhile, quietly waiting for our attention, in almost a thousand locations across Pennsylvania, are millions of items created by our ancestors. Photographs, journals, diaries, letters, ledgers, and government records and more, are all stored, organized and carefully preserved in archives.

What do I mean by archive?

An archive is a collection of unique historical materials preserved and available for research. The materials are typically documents such as books, manuscripts, journals, diaries, letters, ledgers, and business or government records.

How does an archive differ from a library?

A library is a collection of books, movies, music and other published materials available for borrowing to library card holders. Library users take items home for a specific period of time and then return them to the library. The materials are typically recent publications, and multiple copies are available. Library materials are also able to be replaced if damaged or lost. Libraries have a complete catalog of everything in their collection, and it is easily searchable in a computer database by author, title, topic, or category.

In archives, items remain in the archives and do not leave the building. Archival collections are also not as easily searchable which will be covered more in Chapter 3: Using Catalogs and Finding Aids. Archives are the places where we store materials from our past, which are precious to us. They provide one-of-a-kind genealogical sources of our ancestors and are invaluable for research.

Why do I call so many places an "archive?"

Some readers of this book may quibble with the use of the word "archive" for all the places I have listed. Throughout the writing of this book, I could hear statements such as: "*Don't you know that archives are run by professional archivists and those local organizations with their volunteers are not archives?*" and "*The term you should be using is repository.*"

My response is as follows: Local genealogical societies and historical organizations have done more to preserve the history of the peoples of Pennsylvania than most "official" positions has ever done. In fact, some of the largest record loss we have experienced as a state has been through government offices putting historical records in trash dumpsters once they were transcribed, microfilmed, or digitized. Later, people realized that the records which were discarded were not transcribed completely, the microfilm was damaged, or the digital files were corrupted. Anyone saving history is an archivist.

Local community volunteers and family historians preserving their own heritage do not throw out anything from the past. They preserve and care for their history as much or more than institutions have done. To dismiss, denigrate, or ignore the over 800 local archives around the state is to completely miss out on the best Pennsylvania has to offer.

The history of genealogy in America has been a practice of classism, sorting people based on their "pedigree". Those who labeled themselves the best pedigree, worked hard to erase the history of people they considered "low status". Fortunately, thanks to dedicated individuals who hid records from the fanatics, we still have archival records for research. But this drive to destroy the past is ever present, and I am opposed to all efforts to eliminate, or even to edit, historical records.

How this book is organized

My intention for readers of this book is to feel empowered to research in any archive in Pennsylvania. The method and techniques you learn here can be transferred to any archive in the world. The planning, thought process, and considerations are similar no matter the geographic location.

Chapter 1 gives examples of four different types of archival collections in Pennsylvania that can help you in your research. There are images and explanations of how to search these documents and what they can tell you.

Chapters 2 through 4 cover a step-by-step process on how to research in archives. You will learn how to create a plan, use catalogs and finding aids, then make the trip to the archive. If you cannot visit an archive in person, do not fret! You will learn how to request research from home too.

Chapters 5 through 11 are all the archives in Pennsylvania organized by the focus of their collections. The archives are also then organized by the geographic area where each is located. Each chapter begins with background information on the type of collections made by the archives in the chapter, followed by listings of those archives.

Chapter 12 focuses on wrapping-up archival research and discusses copyright, publishing considerations, and organizing your files. An entire book could be written on the steps mentioned here, so take this as a starting point.

Lastly, be sure to check out the bonus materials at the end of the book. The forms included will help you work through a research problem and determine which archives would help you most.

Everything in this book, including website links, is accurate as of November 2024. Endnotes are provided at the end of each chapter, rather than at the end of the book, so they are easier to reference. The images and examples used in the book are from my own archival research and intended as examples of what is possible to find in records, not a prescriptive order of what any one person should research. As with all genealogy research, there is no guarantee of what can be found by any researcher in any archive, and anyone taking on archival research does so with this understanding.

The process of creating this book

Researching and writing this book took place over several years. The chapters on how to research were all originally written as articles on my website, paancestors.com. Readers of the *PA Ancestors Discoveries* newsletter may also recognize portions of these chapters from the newsletter. The listing of the archives themselves were compiled during the shutdowns of the Covid pandemic.

I delayed publishing this book until 2023 after archives re-opened. Many archives were closed to researchers for over two years from March 2020 until summer 2022 or longer. When they re-opened, it was with half the research hours, and appointments required weeks to months in advance. Researchers have also been affected by the move of The Pennsylvania State Archives to a new building and the extensive renovation of the State Library of Pennsylvania. I look forward to a day when archives can return to pre-Covid accessibility.

I am grateful for my family's support throughout the creation of this book. Matt, Cassie, and Elle heard many fun facts about archives around Pennsylvania at dinner each evening. My family is also considerate of the number of hours it takes to produce something like a book. Many nights and weekends were "Mom is writing her book now."

While I followed the process in writing my first book, *Pennsylvania Vital Records Research*, I still struggled to get it to the finish line. Thank you to PA Ancestors Members Janet and Kathleen for being beta-readers of the first draft. Your comments and suggestions made this a better book. My editor Gaynor Haliday corrects all my grammar and style and makes my writing shine. I appreciate her patient and deliberative work.

Writing takes a level of discipline and commitment that I never knew until last year. Growing up, I was the kind of student who never really studied in school and threw together writing assignments in frantic all-nighters. Now in my second spring of life, I am the kind of person who is spending months creating books. Transforming into this person later in life has been a welcome surprise.

Thank you for purchasing and reading *Archives of Pennsylvania*. I love to hear from readers, and can be reached at **hello@paancestors.com**. If this book has helped you in any way, I would appreciate you sharing it on Amazon or Goodreads. Authentic reviews help other genealogists find the book.

For more help in your Pennsylvania genealogy research, sign-up for my free course on Pennsylvania genealogy at **https://welcome.paancestors.com/** .

Denyse

2nd edition, 24 November 2024

Chapter 1

What You Can Find in Archives

THERE ARE MILLIONS OF historical records online today. By typing in a few words into a search bar, we can instantly view links to thousands of possible results.

For genealogists this has been a boon to research. We can go back farther, faster than our parents and grandparents could ever dream.

But not every record of our ancestors is online and easily searchable. According to archivists, it never will be. For every historical document we can view online for an ancestor, there are hundreds to thousands of others in archival boxes around the country. Knowing how to research in archives is an important skill and archives are more accessible than ever.

This chapter will give four examples of archival collections you can search in Pennsylvania, and the types of information you can obtain from them.

Family Letters

Any family historian who received letters passed down in her family will tell you it is one of her most treasured items. If you are looking for letters from your family to others, it is possible there is an archive in Pennsylvania with them. But even if you find no family letters written by one of your ancestors, you may find your ancestors the topic of a letter.

Letters written between family members contained news, not only of the of the family itself, but also the news of what was happening in the community. This letter below was written by Sarah Knox to her brother William while he was in medical school.[1] In it, she tells of two events which occurred in the week prior to April 15, 1850, in Brownsville, PA.

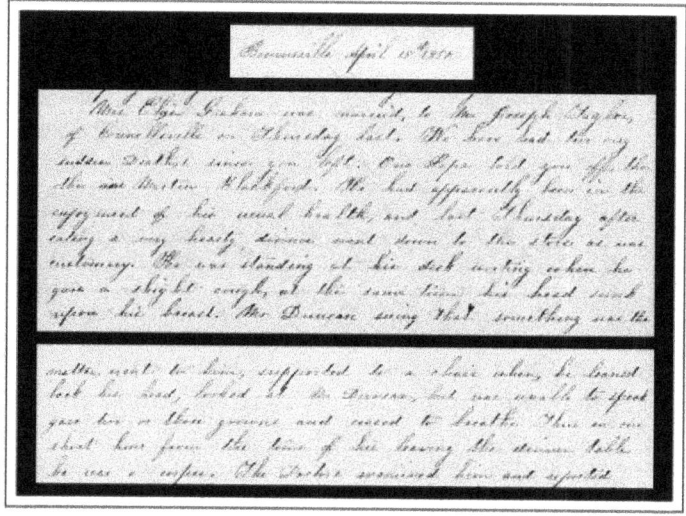

Here is the transcription of the part of the letter shown above:

> *Mrs. Eliza Graham was married to Mr. Joseph Taylor of Connellsville on Thursday last. We have had two very sudden deaths since you left. One Papa told you off [sic], the other was Mister Blackford. He had apparently been in the enjoyment of his usual health, and last Thursday after eating a very hearty dinner went down to the store as was customary. He was standing at his desk writing when he gave a slight cough, at the same time his head sunk upon his breast. Mr. Duncan seeing that something was the matter, went to him, supported to a chair when, he leaned back his head, looked at Mr. Duncan, but was unable to speak, gave two or three groans and ceased to breathe. There in one short hour from the of his leaving the dinner table, he was a corpse.*

The level of detail Sarah provided was better than anything that would be found in a newspaper or vital record! If you have ancestors who lived in Brownsville in the 1850s, their lives may have been discussed in the letters of the Knox family.

Many such collections of family letters are preserved in archives around the state. The key to finding letters useful to your research is locating letters written from a particular time and place. Chapter 2: Creating Your Plan for Archival Research will help you focus your search. Even when you are not descended from the writers of letters, these family letters can reveal details of your ancestors that you will not find anywhere else.

Iron Furnace Time Books

One of the earliest industries in Pennsylvania was mining iron ore and casting it into household products. The workers would first create charcoal from trees over several weeks, then use that charcoal to power furnaces. Mined ore would be purified in the furnaces and cast into products such as stove plates, cookware, and rifle parts.

Iron production was labor intensive and each site, called a plantation at that time, had forty to two hundred workers. These men lived on-site, often in provided housing, with their wives and children. The owner of the iron-making facility was called the "iron master" and he employed a clerk to keep a series of ledger books tracking production, hours worked, and cost of goods sold.

The first iron furnaces began around 1700 and hit their peak production in the 1840s through 1860s with the War with Mexico and Civil War. They rapidly declined post-Civil War as coal-fired furnaces took over the processing of iron into steel products.

These iron furnace time books are helpful for genealogists tracking ancestors from the early 1700s through 1890. Each two-page spread of a time book lists the name of all the workers on-site and the days of the month in a grid. The images below are from the Centre Furnace in Centre County.[2] Each day a person worked is marked, so it is obvious when a worker is no longer employed at that location. This is like a daily census of this one small community.

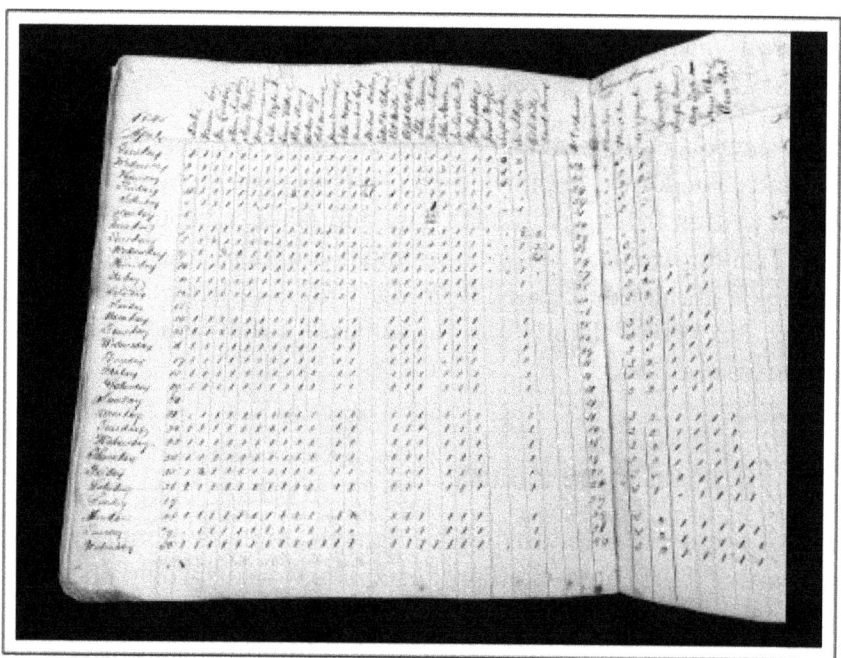

The clerk also made notes alongside the grid to provide details on the workers. This is where a genealogist can get information on an ancestor, such as the type of work he did. The clerk also wrote about time off needed for weddings, funerals, and illness of family members. Prior to 1850, these are often the only record of marriage and death, besides church records.

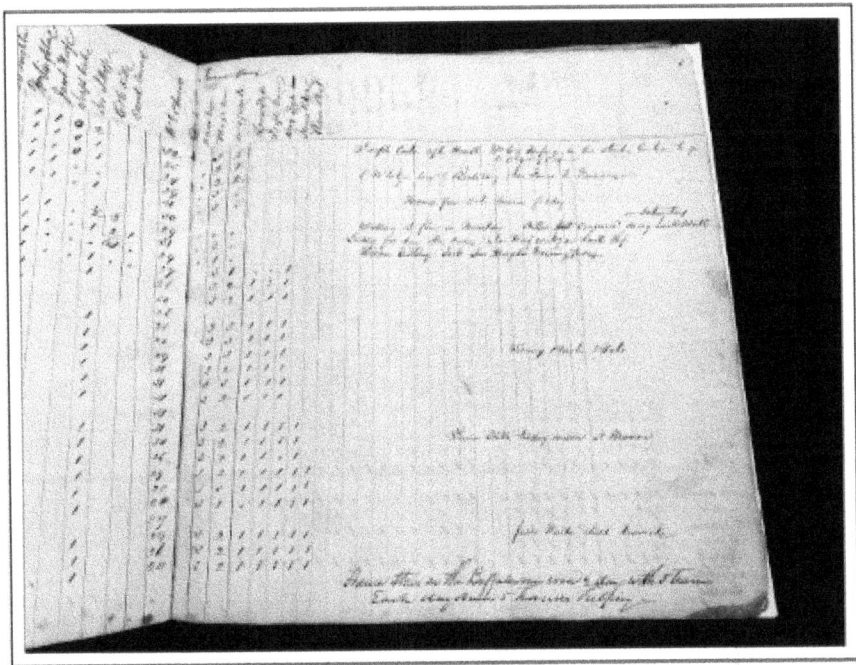

The information in iron furnace records gives a unique glimpse into both the work and personal life of our eighteenth and nineteenth century ancestors. Chapter 6: Regional Pennsylvania Archives and Chapter 7: State-Wide Archives discusses where to find collections of these iron furnace records.

Store Keeper Ledgers

Every community in Pennsylvania had several stores where residents could buy household items. The store owner would track the purchases made by each individual, noting the item, cost, and date of purchase. These ledgers act as a type of constant listing of who lived in the area around the store. Below is an image from a page from the Pinegrove Mills Store in Centre County:[3]

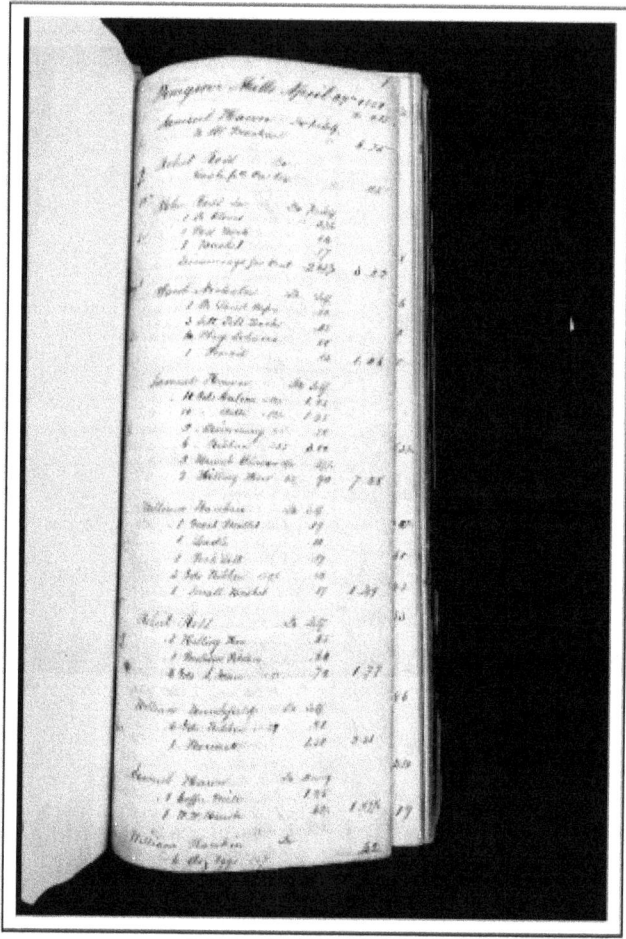

Examining what they purchased also provides a mental image of what their home looked like, what they wore, what they ate, and what daily life was like.

This is a transcription of the page image above. On April 29, 1851 the following people visited the store and purchased these items:

1. *Samuel Hawn – 1/2 bbl. Mackerel*

2. *Robert Ross – Cash pd. Carters*

3. *John Ross Sr. – 1 Pr. Gloves, 1 Pass Book, 1 Basket, Trimmings for a Coat*

4. *Jacob Nicholas – 1 Dr. Sand Paper, 3 Sett Till Locks, 1 Plug*

Tobacco, 1 Pencil

5. *Samuel Hawn – 10 Yds. Calico, 10 Yds. Calico, 2 Yds. Trimming, 6 Yds. Ribbon, 2 Bunch Flowers, 2 Hilling Hocs*

6. *William Rankin – 1 Meat Mallet, 1 Ladle, 1 Peck Salt, 3 Yds. Ribbon, 1 Small Basket*

7. *Robert Ross – 1 Hilling Hock, 1 Molasses Pitcher, 4 Yds. S.Ware*

8. *William Burchfield – 3 Yds. Ribbon, 1 Bonnett*

9. *Samuel Hawn – 1 Coffee Mill, 1 W.W. Brush*

10. *William Rankin – 6 doz. Eggs*

Some of these items and measurements are known in the modern world, such as "Yds. Calico" for yards of calico fabric. Other items are completely foreign, such "W.W. Brush" and "Hilling Hock". These provide opportunities for additional research and to learn more about how one's ancestors lived.

Even if you do not find your particular ancestor, the information from store ledgers can fill in gaps of knowledge when writing a detailed family history. Chapter 3: Using Catalogs and Finding Aids will help you locate these records for your research.

Institutional Records

Institutionalizing people for mental or health reasons was normal in the nineteenth century and first half of the twentieth century. The names for these institutions included "lunatic asylum," "insane asylum," and "state hospital." Pennsylvania hit peak population in its state hospitals in 1950, and many institutions closed in the 1980s. The records of the patients, or inmates as they were known then, are detailed and provide information of great interest for genealogical research and descendants.

This Norristown State Hospital record from 1944 for Charles Geiger is over forty pages long.[4] One part details family interviews which provided information on all of Charles' living relatives. Their marital status, health status, location, and occupations are all listed. This kind of information is rare to find all in one place and is essential for tracing descendants of ancestors to match to shared DNA matches.

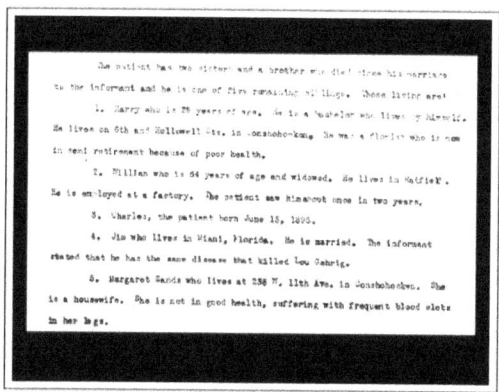

Other parts detail medical diagnoses for Charles which would be of interest to genetic descendants in the case of inheritable conditions. A physician noted that Charles had both Parkinson's disease and several heart conditions. All of these can be passed to descendants.

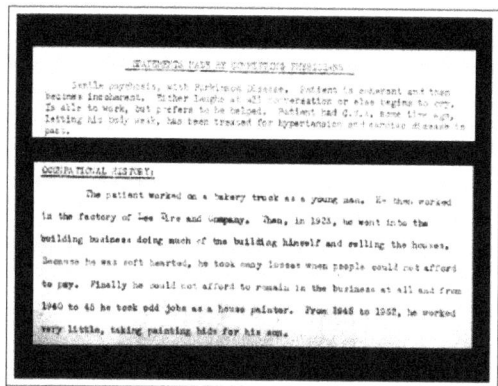

Charles' work history and all his employers are listed as well as what he liked to do for fun at night and weekends. A full picture emerges of what an individual's day-to-day was like.

Records from the nineteenth century are not as detailed as the mid-twentieth century, but they still provide valuable genealogical information. This record of admission to the Danville State Hospital from 1893 for John Toner lists the name and location of his spouse (including the detail that they were separated at the time), and all his children.[5] It also notes that he has no living siblings and his parents are both deceased. Information like this is essential to distinguishing same named individuals and confirming family relationships in a time before birth certificates, death certificates, or marriage licenses.

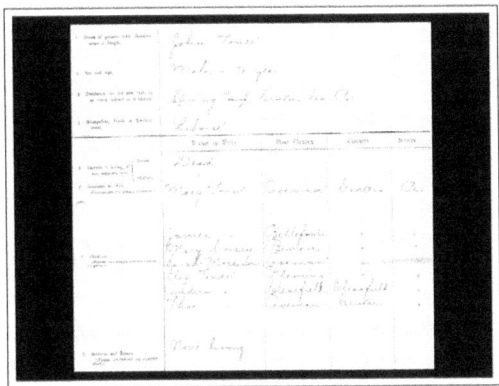

The surviving state hospital records are stored at The Pennsylvania State Archives and are available by a research request by mail. Chapter 4: Researching in Archives in Person or From a Distance will help you in composing that mail-in request.

All the items shared in this chapter are only found in archives and are unlikely to ever be fully digitized and indexed on the internet.

Read on for how you can develop your plan to find archival materials to finish your family tree.

---

1. "William F. Knox Papers, 1829-1863," Correspondence January–June 1850, Darlington Collection, call no. DAR.1949.02, Archives & Special Collections, University of Pittsburgh Library System, Pittsburgh, PA.

2. "Centre Furnace record series 1: Centre Furnace Time Book (1836-1845)," call no. 1478, Eberly Family Special Collections Library, Penn State University Libraries, University Park, PA.

3. "Springfield Mills Store; Milesburg Store: Daybook; Daybook, 045 (1859-1863); 1863-1868," Collection of business and financial books from Central Pennsylvania, call no. 1473, Eberly Family Special Collections Library, Penn State University Libraries, University Park, PA.

4. "Norristown State Hospital Death and Discharge," microfilm, Charles F. Geiger, file no. 41638, Records of Admissions, Discharges, and Deaths at State Institutions, RG 23: Records of the Department of Human Services, Pennsylvania State Archives, Harrisburg, PA.

5. "Danville State Hospital 1904 Admissions," John Toner, file no. 6416, Records of Admissions, Discharges, and Deaths at State Institutions, RG 23: Records of the Department of Human Services, Board of Public Charities Committee on Lunacy; Pennsylvania State Archives, Harrisburg, PA.

Chapter 2

Creating Your Plan for Archival Research

Now that you know some of the items you can find in an archive, it is time to plan your research. In this chapter we will cover how archives came to be and how to craft your research approach.

How Archives Came to Be

Around the turn of the 20th century in the United States, we created a distinction between "libraries" and "archives." In most state capitols and universities, there were libraries which had items they put in "special collections." These special collections were not like the items in the lending part of the library. They were items that were often irreplaceable, unique, and of special historical significance.

For instance, beginning in 1878, State Librarian of Pennsylvania Dr. Charles Ehrenfeld, collected both contemporary newspapers from around the state as well as newspapers printed decades earlier. His initiative provided those in Harrisburg access to news from every county in Pennsylvania, but it also archived thousands of newspapers. The result today is the most extensive and complete collection of Pennsylvania newspapers found anywhere, including the Library of Congress.

By 1900, it was evident that these special collections in libraries needed particular skills for preservation and organization. At the same time, the federal government and most state governments recognized the need for an archive of their documents. Thousands of institutions across the country developed archives between 1900 and 1940. Soon after, a program of training began for archivists to manage these collections.

Archivists are professionals trained in the preservation, description, and cataloging of archival materials. Over the last hundred years, the standards and practices have evolved over how items are described, cataloged, and preserved. Perhaps the best example of this evolution of practices is the use of white cotton gloves to handle archival materials. The use of white gloves was encouraged so that the natural oils on people's hands did not damage the fragile paper. However, after several decades of the practice, archivists realized that the gloves prevented the careful handling of vintage paper, and it was more likely the fragile paper would be torn. Science further supported archivists in showing that freshly washed hands provided no further damage to vintage paper. They changed their recommendation to no cotton gloves needed for handling documents (You will still see television shows showing researchers wearing white gloves while handling paper.).

Two recent changes happened to archival practices in 2021 during the pandemic. The first was the use of hand sanitizer before handling any materials due to the belief that viruses lived on paper. It was soon discovered that the alcohol in hand sanitizer would "eat" or dissolve vintage paper. Fortunately, the practice of hand sanitizer stopped by 2022, but it is not known how much damage was done. The second change in archival practices continues today and involves the descriptors used in archival catalogs. Words used in collection titles and descriptions are regularly evaluated by archivists, then changed if deemed offensive. For researchers this means that we will not be able to find materials under their previously known names, and we must re-search for them all over again.

The practices and standards of archival work are continually evolving. The Society of American Archivists found at **https://www2.archivists.org** communicates and educates on changes in the field.

Now that you have some background information on archives, let's discuss how to approach research in them.

Why You Need a Research Question

Much has been written about crafting research questions to focus your research. This section repeats many of these best practices and provides some additional tips for archival research.

To maximize success, researchers write research questions prior to starting.

Without writing a research question, what typically happens when researchers begin is the equivalent of Alice chasing the White Rabbit down into the rabbit hole. Items will capture the researcher's attention and they are off and running, never stopping to assess what should be looked at. There is no focus, no list of sources, and no capture of what was found. Occasionally, serendipity helps these rabbit-chasing researchers, and they end up making interesting finds, but hours are lost to the chase.

Writing research questions leads to successful research because it defines the research goal. Success in research can look like finding the information you wanted in the record you pulled, or confirming the information you wanted is not in the record you pulled. Success can also look like a thorough search with all name variations, events, topics, locations, and/or dates.

Successful research is about following a carefully planned research process, not the outcome itself.

Researchers also craft research questions before requesting research be completed on their behalf by either the archive staff or a researcher for hire. You must provide clear directions and focus for others if you want results to move your research forward. Being vague and indecisive will leave you disappointed and frustrated with what is returned to you.

Remember, you need focus, not hopping around, to move your genealogy research forward. Focus means step-by-step confirmation of the existence of a record (or not) and getting copies of that record. Step one of focus is crafting a research question.

Crafting Your Research Question

As a genealogist, you have questions like this you are trying to answer:

- Was Mary Jones the daughter of Elizabeth Jones?
- Is Mary Jones the wife of John Smith?
- Who are the parents of John Smith?

Questions like these require a lot of research! Why? Because they are too broad to answer. None of them name the time period or specific location of these individuals. An archive or genealogical society who receives a question like those above will not be able to answer it well, if at all.

Crafting a research question that is targeted and specific takes less than ten minutes. You will use what you already know about your ancestor as the starting point. The things you need to write your research question are:

- The full name of the person and various spellings of their full name, plus any nicknames they could have had.
- Listing known relatives, especially for ancestors with common surnames and given names.
- The location the person lived in, and the locations he or she came from or relocated to (if applicable).
- The length of years, months, or days for the focus of your research question.

Why all these details? You want to make sure you distinguish your Mary Jones from other Mary Jones alive at the same time. It seems to be a truism in genealogy that no matter how low the population in any given area, there are always at least two individuals of the same name and age in that location.

If you don't have exact birth and death dates, be sure to include possible years in a range. If you don't have an exact place, you will need to focus in on one county in Pennsylvania at a time, and preferably a specific township or city in that county. When researching in Philadelphia, you will want to know the exact ward the person resided.

I have developed the template *Research Focus* to help you in crafting your research question. You can download it at **https://www.paancestors.com/book-bonuses/**. Resources to help you with spelling variations and location names are in the back of this book in the *Sources* section.

Returning to the crafting of the research questions above, here are revisions to each one, bringing in specific details of locations and dates:

- Was Mary Jones, born between 1820 and 1825 in Plymouth Township, Montgomery County, the daughter of Elizabeth Jones, born 1790–1798 in same place?

- Was Mary Jones, born between 1820 and 1825 in Plymouth Township, Montgomery County and died 1873 in the same place, the wife of John Smith, born 1822 in England and died in 1864 in the Civil War?

- Who are the parents of John Smith, brother of George Smith (1824–1878), who was born in 1822 in England and died in 1864 in the Civil War?

Each of these revised research questions focuses the research on one specific individual. Each person is named in relationship to other people, a location is given for each one, and dates are given to narrow the search.

Keep refining your research question until it has all of these essential parts:

- Name with alternate spellings

- Exact date or date ranges

- Location as specific as you can make it

You do not have to research only people. You can also focus on events, organizations, and locations.

Researching Events, Organizations, and Locations

You can research an event, organization, or location as your focus, instead of individual people. To do so, craft your research question following the steps above inserting the event, organization, or location in place of the person. Be specific with the time period and do not forget alternative or historical names for places. For example, battles during the Civil War had different names depending on if the history was recorded by the Confederate states or the Union states. You will want both names in your research question, plus what the area is called today if it changed.

Once you have your research question crafted, the next step is to examine archives' catalogs and finding aids for materials to research.

Remember you can download the *Research Focus* free template to help you in crafting your research question at **https://www.paancestors.com/book-bonuses**.

Chapter 3

Using Catalogs and Finding Aids

ONE OF THE MOST challenging jobs for archivists — professional or volunteer — is cataloging their collections. Every item needs to be given a title or name, creator, date, location, and at least some short description. When materials arrive at an archive, they rarely come with a full history of why they were created and by whom and for what purpose. Archivists are continually challenged by how to describe their collections.

To understand the complexity, let's compare collections in archives to published books in libraries.

Published books, housed in libraries, come to the library with title, category, author, and creation date already established by the publisher. Books also have short descriptions called "blurbs" describing their contents on the back cover. Librarians can quickly add new books to their collections, and everything is easily searchable by title, author, category, and description. In addition, published books are organized the same way in every library in the country. You will not find Stephen King's epic horror novel *Children of the Corn* in fiction in one library, and in history in another.

Let's cover how archives are organized and an approach to using them by developing a research profile.

How Archives are Organized

Each archive develops its own organization system to best preserve and access its specific collections. While national organizations, such at the Society of Archivists, recommend standards and practices, it is ultimately up to each archive to decide what they collect and how to catalog it. Researchers will find a broad spectrum across our institutions in the state.

At the most basic level, archives will organize the items they hold into collections. Each collection will have a title describing what is in it, such as "Postcards of the Wyoming Valley". Usually the description is accompanied by a date and creator of the items. In larger institutions, particularly government and university archives, collections further described by record groups (RG), categories, and type of item, such as photograph, loose papers, book, map, etc.

This process of organizing and describing archival items is called cataloging. There are three challenges with cataloging archival items: meeting standards, donation volume, and lack of indexing.

Government archives and university archives employ archivists trained in the standards of cataloging. Unfortunately, most of the state's local archives listed in Chapter 9, cannot afford to pay for professionally trained archivists to do cataloging. Catalogs, and even inventories of exactly what a local archive holds, are often lacking details or are nonexistent.

There has been growing recognition of the value of local archive collections. The Historical Society of Pennsylvania's project Hidden Collections Initiative for Pennsylvania Small Archival Repositories sent professional archivists around to local archives in and around Philadelphia to learn what was at each one. Results of their cataloging can be found at the Historical Society of Pennsylvania's website at **https://hsp.org/historical-heritage-organizations/hidden-collections-initiative-for-pennsylvania-small-archival-repositories/subject-guide** and also on the Philadelphia Area Archives Research Portal (PAARP) at **https://findingaids.library.upenn.edu**.

In addition to the challenge of describing items so they can cataloged, there is also the issue of the volume of archival items to be processed. This might be shocking to read, but not everything in even highly-staffed archives is cataloged. Donated collections are always coming in, and it takes months to years to process each one. Every archival repository has piles of historical materials awaiting cataloging. To process materials, collections may have been quickly described with just a few words, such as "Correspondence, 1822–1864." Details such as who are in the letters or the subjects discussed are not in the catalog.

One type of cataloging that is almost never done in archival records is indexing. Indexing is the process of going through every piece of an archival collection and noting the names, dates, and places on each item, then making all that information searchable in the catalog. For example, indexing is found in non-fiction books, so readers can search for topics of interest, then turn to the exact page with that topic. A book without an index means someone must read the entire book to find that topic. Another example of the value of indexing is records on genealogy websites. Digital images are tagged in the metadata with names, dates, and places, and that meta data is searchable in the website's computerized index. Genealogists can quickly add facts (the meta data) and images to their family trees through the power of indexing.

These challenges of cataloging historical items is why researchers often make revelatory discoveries in archival collections. One such discovery was made at the National Archives in Washington D.C. in 2021. A listing of families in Alaska for the 1890 census was cataloged by archives in the 1960s.[1] The listings were in a census enumerator's logbook, one of the few surviving records of the 1890 census. This logbook was stored for sixty years before a researcher found the precious information. Stories like this are a good reminder that any person who carefully goes through an archival collection has the possibility of discovering a piece of history thought to be lost forever.

If you are a researcher who would like to make big discoveries about the past, you need to learn how to navigate archive catalogs, and the catalogs' cousin: the finding aid.

Types of Archive Catalogs

Every archive, genealogical or historical society, or library has a website. Most of these places also have some form of online catalog or a listing of the types of sources available for research. The catalog and sources listings will provide a broad idea of the type of materials in that archive, such as maps, photographs, church records, and the topics or subjects of focus for each, such as maps of the Coal Region, aerial photographs of the 1950s, and specific religious congregations.

Examining archive catalogs will inform you as to their usefulness for answering your research question. Unfortunately, there is no master list of archival catalogs, and no two archives have the same format for their catalog. Researchers have to visit each archive's catalog on their website, and navigate it.

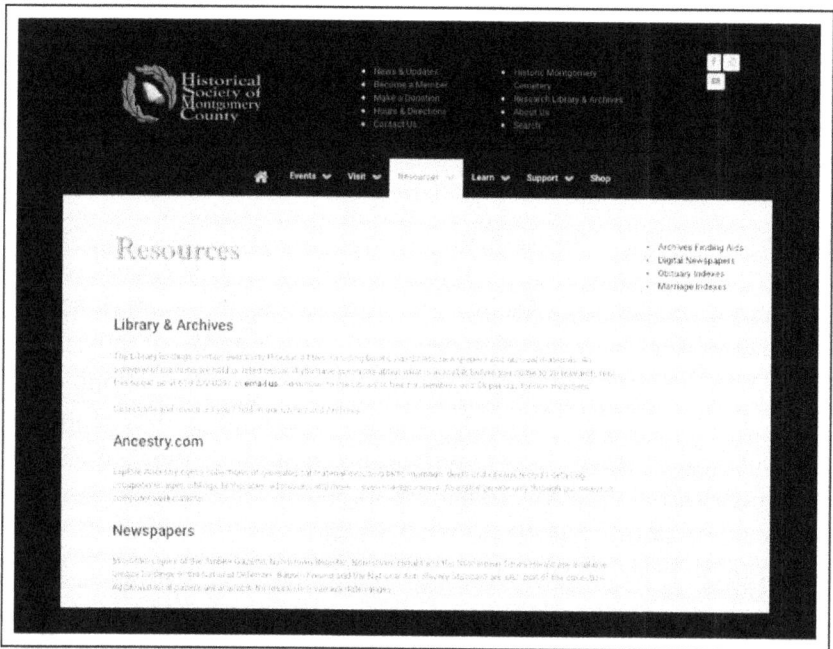

Website: https://hsmcpa.org/index.php/resources/library-archives

Local organizations tend to have the most simplistic catalog for archival materials, if they have one at all. In place of a full catalog, they may provide a listing of types of collections, such as maps, scrapbooks, photographs, vertical files, family papers. One example is the Historical Society of Montgomery County. On its website there is a listing of the types of sources available for research.

On another webpage, the Society website provides a way to do a basic search of the titles of items in their collections. As with almost every archival collection, the ability to search every name in collections is not available, but a researcher will have an idea of the types of records on site.

For larger institutional archives, such as the Pennsylvania State Archives, the catalog is organized in a hierarchy.

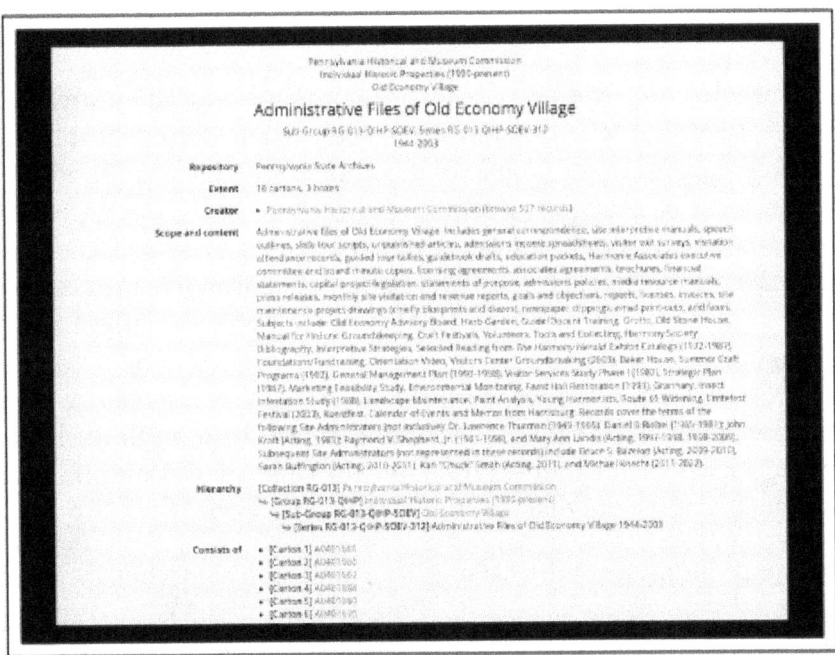

Website:
https://gencat.eloquent-systems.com/pennsylvania-state-archives/permalink.html?key=coll9910

The first level is the Record Group, and for the State Archives this is the government department, agency, or office who created those records. The next levels get more and more specific, narrowing archival items into boxes and folders based by location, date, subject, or numbers.

Boxes and folders are barcoded with unique numbers. When a box is pulled off the storage shelves for research, the barcode identifies the box as the one in the catalog. The shelf location also has a unique tag, so items are returned to their correct location. Details like this are important when there are tens of millions of items in archival storage.

In the 2020s, not everything in an archive started as papers. In the twenty-first century, some items in archives are digital-only.

The challenge of born-digital materials

The biggest change in the archival world has been in the last two decades with the preservation of 'born-digital' materials.

Today we live in a world where some of our most crucial information and records never take physical form, such as a paper application or signed document. One example of this is the United States President's Twitter (now X) account. Beginning with President Obama, it was common for the President to tweet out policy decisions or reactions to national or international events. The National Archives had to develop a plan to preserve social media posts, not just for the President, but for all federal officials. These social media posts also needed to be cataloged and accessible for research. Born-digital materials preservation is an immense project that many archives are currently working through. We as genealogists might want to think of the same preservation for our social media posts, but that is a topic for another book.

Not everything in an archive catalog has a finding aid, but when there is a finding aid, you will want to use it. These documents are key to learning what is in a collection and determining if it is worth researching.

Archival Finding Aids

A finding aid is detailed listing of one archival collection's contents. It still is not an index of every name and location in the collection, but it is more specific than a catalog entry alone. Ideally, every archival collection has a finding aid, but usually it is only popular collections or collections of wealthy donors.

Finding aids are usually written to be printed out on letter-size, 8 1/2 x 11-inch paper. They range in length from a few pages to hundreds of pages. When finding aids are in PDF form, they can be downloaded and searched using the built-in search tool in every PDF reader. I suggest downloading any finding aids you find useful because you can easily search them and annotate directly on the PDF with your own notes.

Finding aids, like catalogs, come in a variety of formats. Generally, finding aids are organized into the following sections:

- Title of the collection
- Narrative background of how it was created and obtained
- Historical context of the subject of the collection
- Subjects or topics within the collections
- Date ranges of the collection
- Organization into boxes and folders with topics and or dates for each
- Related collections in that archive (and occasionally other archives)

The example below is a several decades old finding aid from The Pennsylvania State Archives for the Harmony Society. The Harmony Society was a religious group founded in 1805 who lived communally in Economy Village in Butler County. This finding aid is for one small part of the collection. You can see that the topic of each part of the collection is named, along with the box and folder number where to find it.

```
                         MG-437
                   KARL ARNDT COLLECTION
            Administrative File, 1805-1905 (Not Incl)

SUBJECT                                          FOLDER #   BOX #
  1819/6/19  List of Members of the Harmony                         Roll 1
             Society                                1         1      5153
  1821       Articles of Association (copy)         2
  1821       Articles of Association                3
  c.1825     List of members of the Harmony Society
             with date of death, age, and date of
             joining the Society                    4
  1805,1827  Articles of Association                5
  c.1831     Register of births                     6
  1832/2/20  By Laws Adopted by the Harmony
             Society                                7         1
  1832/2/21  Election of Council of Elders
  1834/7/5   Appointment of George Rapp as General
             Agent                                  8
  c.1835     Register of births                     9
  1841/2/26  Articles of Association (Johann Gottlieb
             Loisa Frederika Muntz)                10
  c.1842     Register of births of female members  11
  c.1846     List of male members with date of death,
             age, date of arrival, and years with the
             society                               12
  1805, 1826, 1836, 1847  Bereinigungs-Artikel DER
             Harmonie-Gesellschaft [PRINTED]       13
  1848/10/26 Jacob Henrici Letter of Resignation   14
  1861       List of members                       15
  1865       List of households of Harmony Society 16
```

Website:
http://www.phmc.state.pa.us/bah/dam/mg/ys/m437ys1Pt1.pdf

In summary, examine the catalog, finding aids, and listing of materials to determine if they have the records you need. Ask yourself:

- Do they have records for the location and time period you are focusing on?

- Are any of the people you are searching (or their family, associates, and neighbors) listed in the catalog?

- Have you looked for collections of materials of religions, clubs, associations, and employers of your research subject?

If you aren't finding what you want, contact other genealogy researchers to ask for advice. Also contact the archives and ask for help in locating collections based on what you desire. Archivists know each other and have their own networks, so they may be able to help you find what you seek in another archive.

Now that you know how archives are organized with catalogs and finding aids, it is time to shift into archival research mode. This mode of researching is completely different than researching on genealogy websites.

Shifting Your Mindset

To begin researching in archive catalogs, the initial step is not one of skill but of mindset.

Archival research has a different pace than internet searching. There is no place in an archive where you can enter a few words and get instant answers. Pause for a few moments and tell yourself you are going to move slowly and carefully before you begin. Genealogist J. Mark Lowe infamously uses the phrase "mull and ponder" in his presentations, conjuring a vision of walking along a park path, hands behind one's back, deep in thought. You may also find it helpful to think of fictional detectives Nancy Drew or Hercule Poirot. Both these characters spent most of their time solving a mystery by deliberately collecting information and examining evidence. Use whatever works for you to consciously shift yourself to slow mode.

Another mindset shift is think of connections, instead of in keywords. The internet trained us to get some pieces of a collection by entering a few words. In archives, we are examining an entire collection of someone's whole life or work, or a whole company or place. You may find it helpful to imagine yourself living in the time period and place your ancestors lived in. Picture what life was like for them on any given day of the year. Who did they interact with? Neighbors? Store keepers? Mill operator? Factory boss? Minister of their church? What did they do at their county courthouse each year or over their life? Pay taxes? Serve on juries? Transfer a deed? Complete probate proceeding for deceased family? Complete the paperwork to become a citizen? Just imagine as best you can what life was like for them when they lived. Mull and ponder and make notes of all your thoughts and questions.

Now you are in the best mindset for archive research and can make your ancestor's research profile.

Create the Research Profile

When you begin to research in archive catalogs (if one exists at the archive), you will not be able to type names into search bars and get instant links to exact document images. Your search will start with what you know about your ancestor, so it is best to write it all down. This is called creating a research profile.

The research profile is developed out of the research question you already created (see Chapter 2: Creating Your Plan for Archival Research) and the research you completed so far. You will build your research profile with the following pieces of information on your ancestor:

Location where the ancestor lived

Be as specific as possible, down to the county, municipality, street name, ward, etc. Also note any historical name changes for that geographic location. For example, from 1790 to 1860, new counties in Pennsylvania were formed out of existing, larger counties. Your ancestor who was planted in one spot likely did not move, but the county name changed above him or her.

Years the ancestor lived in that location

Again, be as specific as possible, down to the month if available. If you are later examining something like a transaction in a store keeper's ledger, or a family letter, these dates will matter to prove it was your ancestor and not someone with a similar name.

All the possible spellings of the ancestor's name

Both given name (first name and middle name) and surname (last name) should be listed out in your research notes or research log with all its possible variations. Some of these "misspellings" you found in existing records. Others may have been created and you just have not found them yet! Some resources to help you generate this list of spelling variations is in the back of this book under *Sources*.

Anything else you know about him or her from current records

Look over everything you have collected so far on this ancestor and make a list of characteristics you find. These details are found in original records, including images of those records on websites. Here are some ideas of what to look for in existing records to get you started:

- Religion – can be found in religious records, marriage licenses by researching the officiant, and obituaries.

- Ethnicity – can be assumed from surname and association in fraternal groups.

- Occupation – listed on census, death certificates, and obituaries.

- Political party – noted in biographies and voting records.

- Military service – mentioned in obituaries, county histories, and death certificates.

- Fraternal organization – mentioned in obituaries and newspaper articles, as well as county histories.

- Family and extended family – can be assumed from census records, and found in vital records and obituaries.

- Institutionalization – including prison, asylum, hospital, and orphanage can be found on vital records and newspaper articles.

- Major life events – noting events such war, natural disaster, injury, bankruptcy, divorce, injuries, orphaned, and birth defects can open up avenues for additional sources to search.

Think of this list you are creating as the FAN (Family, Associates, Neighbors) Club in extreme. If you need inspiration for the kinds of finds you could make, review Chapter 1: What You Can Find in an Archive for examples.

Note: Do not discount family lore and tidbits passed down through the years. List it out along with the facts you have from records and note the source.

If you are unsure about some of the above characteristics of the ancestor, it is okay to make a guess based on what you already know. Just note it as a guess in your list. For example, if researching an Irish ancestor who arrived in America in the 1700s, you could assume that person is of Presbyterian faith. Whereas, in 1845 at the height of the Potato Famine, you could guess that ancestor is of Roman Catholic faith because that was the dominant religion of immigrants from Ireland at that time.[2]

To help you collect this information on your ancestor, this book includes a bonus template entitled *Ancestor Profile*. Go to **https://www.paancestors.com/book-bonuses** to download it and all the bonus materials for this book.

---

1. Kluskens, Claire, "An 1890 Census Fragment for Alaska is Rediscovered," *National Archives:Text Message* (https://text-message.blogs.archives.gov/2021/08/31/an-1890-census-fragment-for-alaska-is-rediscovered/), 31 August 2021.

2. "History and Demographics of the Irish Coming to America," *Macauly Honors College at City University of New York (CUNY), (https://www.macaulay.cuny.edu/seminars/gardner-irish/articles/h/i/s/History_and_Demographics_of_the_Irish_Coming_to_America_248e.html)*, 27 April 2009.

Chapter 4

Researching in Archives in Person or From Home

So far you have learned what type of materials are in archives, how to craft a research question, and how to search archive catalogs and finding aids. Now it is finally time to do the actual research!

In this chapter, we will cover how to prepare for a research trip in person and strategies for making the most of your time in an archive. We will also discuss how to make research requests through the mail (or email) to an archive, and how to hire a researcher to research in an archive for you.

Archives are welcoming places, and they want you to use their resources for your research. With some preparation and the right attitude, you can research with confidence, both in person and from home. Surprises and treasures await you in archives.

Research Trips in Person

If you are planning a visit to an archive for genealogy research, you may be wondering how to prepare yourself and what to bring along. It is important to arrive with your essential items, so you can focus during your research time. Whether you are a seasoned researcher or a first-timer, these tips will help you get the most out of your archive visit.

Research the archive's website

Most archives have a website that provides information about their collections, hours of operation, and research policies. It is important to read through this information thoroughly to get a better understanding of what to expect during your visit.

Since the pandemic, most archives require appointments for on-site research. These appointments can be booked out for weeks to months into the future, so be sure to look well in advance of your planned visit.

Also look for the the following information about the archive: available parking, research fees, copying fees (even digital images with a mobile device are charged a fee in some archives), and what devices (phone, tablet, laptop) are allowed inside the research room. Most archives have a locker area where you can leave your outwear, purse, and other personal items before you enter.

Prepare yourself

Archives are not like your average library or bookstore. Researching in an archive can be overwhelming. Not only are you in a new place with unfamiliar rules and procedures, but you are also handling original, historical documents created by your ancestors. It's emotional to touch something created by a relation from hundreds of years ago!

You may also find information that fills you with joy, anger, sadness, or frustration. You do not know what will be revealed as you open those archival boxes and begin to read. Give yourself permission to take breaks, step outside and do a few deep breaths or call a friend if needed.

Practice reading handwriting

Few archival documents are typewritten, so you will be spending most of your time reading handwriting. If you would like to practice reading handwriting prior to your visit, check the *Sources* section in the back of the book for suggestions.

Appropriate clothing and materials for handling documents

Archives can feel cold, with temperature and humidity controls designed to protect delicate materials. It is important to dress appropriately, because no archive will allow you to wear outerwear, scarves, or hats inside research rooms. This clothing limitation is to prevent the theft of materials.

A sweater or cardigan with a shirt underneath works for most people. You may want to wear dark colors, because archival materials are often full of dust, and some are crumbling due to age. This may end up all over the front of you as you turn pages.

You do not need to wear cotton gloves while handling documents, but you may want to bring nitrile gloves (not latex) to keep your hands clean. Most historical documents, and especially leather-bound or fabric-bound ledger books, tend to leave dirt and dust on your hands. You will definitely want to wash your hands when you are done researching for the day.

Contacting the archive in advance

In addition to researching the archive's website and making your appointment, it is also a good idea to contact the archive at least a month prior to your visit. You want to confirm the collections you want are available. Collections are pulled for re-organization, digitization, or various other reasons. This check ahead can be done ahead of time via email or phone.

You may also be able to arrange for materials to be pulled for you in advance of your visit, which can save you time once you arrive. For archives which keep their materials in vault storage, it is common to wait thirty minutes to an hour for materials to arrive in a research room. When you only have a few hours of time in an archive, every minute counts.

This check-in ahead of your visit is also a great opportunity to ask any questions you have about research procedures and policies you studied on the website. Archivists would much rather answer your questions before you arrive, than surprise you with something on the day you arrive.

Necessary identification and archive rules

When visiting an archive, it is important to bring the necessary identification and documentation. This may include a government-issued ID, such as a driver's license or passport. If you are researching at the National Archives, you will also need to apply for a researcher's card on your first visit there.

Most archives require you to fill out a registration form or sign a research agreement before accessing materials. Follow all rules of that archive for document handling, photographs, copies, copyright, etc. The rules vary from archive to archive, but generally the following are universal:

- Registration and Identification – Most archives have researchers sign in at arrival and sign-out and at departure, and show some form of identification.
- No food, drink, gum, or pens – Nothing that could damage historical items are allowed inside.
- No outerwear such as coats, hats, or gloves worn in the research room.
- Request forms – Often materials for research are requested from staff through the completion of a submission form in the research room.

Whatever the rules are at a particular archive, it is important to follow them. Researchers can be banned from the building or escorted out for non-compliance.

Tools for note-taking and saving images

When researching in an archive, it is important to have the right tools for taking notes and saving images of what you found. This may include items like a laptop or tablet for taking digital notes, a notepad and pencil for handwritten notes, and a camera or mobile phone for photographing materials.

Practice using whatever you are bringing along. This is not the time to try out that new mobile app for the first time.

Some repositories have ScanPro microfilm machines which allow you to save the microfilmed images as PDFs on a USB drive. Make sure the drive is empty and you know how to insert it, rename images as you save them, and eject the drive.

More items you may want to bring to an archive

Once you have covered these essentials of a genealogy research trip to an archive, you may want to consider bringing the following items. This is what I personally bring along for a research trip. Not all these items come into the research room, but they are in the archive's locker or in my car and easily accessible if I need them.

- Post-it Notes: These are handy for saving a page in a reference book or paper index onsite, and take notes on a paper copies of archival materials made in archives which do not allow photography. Some archives will not let Post-its into research rooms, so index cards are a good back up.

- Paper fasteners: At repositories which only allow paper copies of their materials, I like to organize those copies right away. I bring plastic paper clips to fasten the copies into relevant bundles.

- Pencils: I bring 3 to 4 pencils pre-sharpened. I have yet to find sharpened pencils waiting for me in a research room. And if I do need to sharpen a pencil, the loud sound the sharpener makes in the research room, makes me cringe.

- Ear plugs: I use these in case the archive is noisy with multiple conversations happening. I prefer to work in silence.

- Reading glasses: I have a second pair packed in my bag just in case. If I cannot read the materials, the trip is a waste of time.

- Tissues and sinus and/or headache medicine: The dust on archival materials makes my nose run, so I am ready with a pack of tissues and something for my sinuses. I also get headaches sometimes, so I bring something for that too.

- Power cables and portable battery chargers: I never want to run out of battery power while taking images of archival documents. Many archives do not have outlets in the research room, so portable battery chargers have saved me a couple times. I also bring power cables to charge my devices in case there is an outlet I can use.

- Microfiber cloth: Used to wipe off my glasses, and phone and tablet screens.

Because I research in archives frequently, I have a briefcase-like bag that I call my "genealogy research bag" which I store all the above items in. I am ready to research anytime!

Taking breaks and managing your time

Researching in an archive can be overwhelming. Each archival collection, and often each folder or box inside a collection, is different. Handwriting changes from document to document, and sometimes the fragile condition of items is nerve wracking. It's important to take breaks and manage your energy.

Many archives have designated break areas where researchers can take step away, and grab a snack or drink. Be sure to plan where you will be having lunch before you arrive. You do not want to spend 30 minutes deciding, then an hour getting there and eating it, and miss your valuable research time. If you can pack your lunch and eat it in the break area, or outside, you can keep your meal break as short as possible.

It is also important to set realistic goals for your research and to prioritize the materials that are most important to your research topic. Have a printed list on paper, plus on the personal device (phone, tablet, or laptop) you bring with you. List the collections you will be researching in order from most important to least important.

In conclusion, genealogy researching in an archive can be a rewarding experience if you come prepared with the right tools and mindset. By researching the archive's website, contacting the archive in advance, and bringing along things to enhance your research, you can make the most of your visit and enjoy discovering the past.

Research Requests Through Mail (or Email)

Genealogy research in person can be a rewarding and a fun reason for travel. However, not everyone has the time, opportunity, or resources to visit archives in person. Fortunately, many archives now offer a convenient option for remote research requests through the mail or email.

A request to any archive, genealogical or historical society, or library, is a request for someone there to look at their onsite records, and make a copy of records and send you that copy. They are not staffed to do anything other than pull records and make copies. If you give them a big research question such as "send me a copy of every Jones' family baptism", you will end up disappointed. Archives staff will likely turn down your request or put it off for several months.

Your steps to prepare your research request through mail (or email) are the same as if you were going to the archive in person to do research. Review Chapter 2: Creating Your Plan for Archival Research and Chapter 3: Using Catalogs and Finding Aids for how to prepare for archival research. You will need to carry out all the steps described so you can give the archive a focused, properly detailed, research request.

Next examine the procedures and fees for taking research requests. Most places have a minimum and maximum number of hours for research, or a specific number of look-up requests they will do. On the research request form, they will ask for details of your request, often asking for what you have already searched. It is important here to be brief and direct. They do not want five paragraphs on about every twist-and-turn of your research over the past ten years. A bullet list of records previously searched is direct and easy to read.

Here is an example of a typical research request from an inexperienced researcher:

I have been researching the Fetterman family for 22 years. The first Fetterman to come to America arrived in 1744 and he lived in Lancaster County. I have previously conducted research at Lancaster History and the Pennsylvania State Archives and included the results of all the records I have found so far. I see on your website that you have church records from the colonial period. I am trying to confirm the children and wife of Johan Fetterman – the first Fetterman to arrive in America. I have so much research on this family already and this part is the last thing I need to do. Your website also tells me that you have church records for the period 1732 to 1825 for 95 different churches in Lancaster County. Do you think church records will help me confirm the children of Johan Fetterman? I have tried to decide, but can not decide, so I would like you to look at any records for Fetterman families you have that could tell me who the children and wife are of Johan Fetterman. I have called and spoken with Sarah at the archives and she says that such research is possible. I have also called three other archives and it seems like you are the one who can help me the most. I am desperate to finish this research and hope you can help me.

Notice how difficult it is to determine what it is this person wants. The request needs to be read several times to understand exactly what is being asked for. The request is also for "any records" and leaves the research completely to the discretion of the archivist or volunteer. The result returned could be almost anything, and possibly something the requester already has.

Here is the same request, re-written based on the advice in this book:

My research question is "Who are the children and spouse of Johan Fetterman, born about 1717 in Germany and died about 1803 in Ohio." I have been unable to locate probate records in Ohio, and land records do not have any children or spouse listed. Tax records show Johan Fetterman in the city of Lancaster, Lancaster County from 1744 to 1785. I am requesting a search of baptism records for the churches in Lancaster city for the Fetterman family from 1744 to 1765. Alternative spellings for Fetterman include Fitterman, Fedderman, and Vedderman.

This research request is clear and to the point. It omits the personal stories in the typical research requests. The key pieces of information needed are all present: name, date range, and location. Alternative surname spellings are included to communicate directly what should be included in the search. And finally, a request for church baptism records is specific and not a wild goose chase through records. An archivist or volunteer looking at this request knows they are helping a researcher who is focused and professional. This kind of request will be completed quickly and easily.

Lastly, keep in mind that every repository and archives receives more requests each day than they can answer. It is normal to wait several weeks for a response. If you follow the tips in this chapter, your research request will be successful in letting you know for certain if the records you want exist or not, and if they do, you will receive a copy.

Hiring a Researcher

My personal experience in hiring researchers to go to archives and make copies of materials, ranges from horrible and expensive to wonderful and worth every penny. I have learned from experience to make clear requests, to ask for recommendations, not make assumptions, and ensure there is a contract detailing specific work and prices.

Be clear – are you hiring a researcher to get archival records for you, or do you have a sticky research problem that needs analysis and expertise? If you want record retrieval (also called "record pulls"), then read on! If you have something more complex, I suggest you go to the Association of Professional Genealogists website and search for a professional to hire. You can search by locality and time period expertise, so you can be sure to connect with people who can help you.

Ask around for recommendations of a researcher you can hire. One place to start is Facebook groups discussing genealogy for the county the archive is located in. Go to Facebook.com and in the search bar type in the name of the county, Pennsylvania (states share a lot of the same county names), and "genealogy" or "genealogical". You will get a list of results of either pages or groups. Use the Facebook Message feature to contact the pages or groups privately for a recommendation, or post it directly for anyone to respond. I also have a list of local genealogical societies for every county in Chapter 9. Searching for new genealogy groups every so often is a good idea, because new ones do form!

The same guidelines for sending requests to an archive directly also apply to sending a research request to a hired researcher. Be clear, direct, and to the point. Leave out the backstory and emotion. The researcher you hire is paid by the hour, and there are only so many hours in a day. Being respectful of their time shows that you are serious about the results they produce.

Do not assume that a researcher knows more than you do about the family you are researching. You are the expert on your family history. He or she may have suggestions for you, and if so, you can discuss those further with the researcher. But the majority of researchers doing record pulls do not have time to deeply analyze and consult on each research request. Archival research is time-consuming to do.

The researcher should provide a simple contract to you stating the number of hours they will spend, their hourly rate for research, the fees for copies, how to access and download digital images, and a guarantee of quality of the images with specific resolution stated. Contracts can have a deposit requested. A deposit assures your contracted researcher that they will be paid and you are serious about your research. The researcher should also state a timeframe in which they will go to the archive and send you the copies or images of the records.

Turn down any offer from a researcher you hired for record retrieval to write a report for you. Genealogy research reports take a minimum of ten hours to complete and could cost $1,000 or more. Make sure the contract you sign limits the number of hours you will pay, or agree to a total amount of dollars you will pay.

Whether you do the research yourself or have someone do it for you, you are now ready to go to an archive. The next six chapters detail the over eight hundred archives in Pennsylvania available for research.

Chapter 5

State-Wide Archives

ARCHIVES IN THIS CHAPTER are those with collections from all geographic areas of Pennsylvania. Two are state government institutions, the Pennsylvania State Archives and the State Library of Pennsylvania; one is operated by the federal government, the National Archives in Philadelphia; and the remainder are privately run. Generally, government-operated archives hold records created by the government, and nothing created by individuals such as journals and letters. However, early in the collecting of historical materials in Pennsylvania's State Archives and State Library, papers of influential individuals were included in these archives. Researchers will also find original state government and county government records at the Historical Society of Pennsylvania. Consider this yet another example of the lack of hard rules in archival organization.

The privately run archives listed here, the Historical Society of Pennsylvania, the Genealogical Society of Pennsylvania, and FamilySearch, are all regularly used by genealogists for research. They are all a "must do" for thorough research in Pennsylvania, no matter where your ancestors were located here.

***

Pennsylvania State Archives

Location: 1681 North Sixth Street, Harrisburg, PA 17120-0090
Telephone: (717) 783-3281
Email: ra-statearchives@pa.gov
Website: https://pastatearchives.com
Catalog: https://www.phmc.pa.gov/Archives/Research-Online

History

The Pennsylvania State Archives collects, preserves and makes available for study the permanently-valuable public records of the Commonwealth, with particular attention given to the records of state government. The State Archives also collects papers of private citizens and organizations relevant to Pennsylvania history.[1]

The Pennsylvania State Archives called 350 North Street, Harrisburg on the state capitol complex its home until 2023. After a decade-long planning and construction endeavor, the Archives completed its relocation to 1681 North Sixth Street, Harrisburg. The new facility offers enhanced research areas, exhibition spaces for archival artifacts, and expanded storage capacity expected to last 50 years.

Among the over 250 million items within the Archives, you will find William Penn's Charter, Pennsylvania's founding document. Although not every item rivals the Charter, each record has earned its place due to its historical, legal, or financial significance to the Commonwealth.

Collections

The Pennsylvania State Archives boasts an extensive collection of 165 million pages of documents, 18,000 microfilm reels, and 1 million special collection items. These holdings span from 1664 to the present day and encompass diverse materials such as photographs, maps, blueprints, motion picture rolls, and audio and video tapes.

Among the treasures safeguarded at the State Archives are the 1681 Charter granted by Great Britain's King Charles II to William Penn, the 1737 Walking Purchase document, photographs of burning of

Chambersburg, Franklin County in 1864, the 1878 Death Warrant for Molly Maguire leader John J. Kehoe, and a letter describing the 1948 Donora smog disaster which killed 20 people and injured thousands. Recently, archivists secured the acquisition of one of the original Minutes of General Assembly from March 16, 1779, a remarkable record detailing Revolutionary War-era deliberations of the Pennsylvania Assembly.

The Archives is organized into governmental records and non-governmental or manuscript collections. The majority of the records are the from various agencies and departments of the state government and organized into the below record groups.

Pennsylvania State Archives Governmental Record Groups

- RG 001 Department of Agriculture
- RG 002 Department of the Auditor General
- RG 003 Civil Service Commission
- RG 004 Office of the Comptroller General
- RG 005 Constitutional Conventions and Council of Censors
- RG 006 Department of Forests and Waters
- RG 007 General Assembly
- RG 008 General Loan Office and State Treasurer
- RG 009 General State Authority
- RG 010 Office of the Governor
- RG 011 Department of Health
- RG 012 Department of Highways
- RG 013 Pennsylvania Historical and Museum Commission
- RG 014 Department of Internal Affairs

- RG 015 Department of Justice
- RG 016 Department of Labor and Industry
- RG 017 Land Office
- RG 018 Loan and Transfer Agent
- RG 019 Department of Military and Veterans' Affairs
- RG 020 Department of General Services
- RG 021 Proprietary Government
- RG 022 Department of Education
- RG 023 Department of Human Services
- RG 024 Office of the Register General
- RG 025 Special Commissions
- RG 026 Department of State
- RG 027 Pennsylvania's Revolutionary Governments
- RG 028 Treasury Department
- RG 029 Pennsylvania Turnpike Commission
- RG 030 Pennsylvania State Police
- RG 031 Department of Commerce
- RG 032 Pennsylvania Liquor Control Board
- RG 033 Supreme Court of Pennsylvania
- RG 034 Department of Community Affairs
- RG 035 Milk Marketing Board
- RG 036 Legislative Reference Bureau
- RG 037 Public Utility Commission

- RG 038 Superior Court
- RG 039 Game Commission
- RG 040 Insurance Department
- RG 041 Navigation Commission for the Delaware River and its Navigable Tributaries
- RG 042 Department of Revenue
- RG 043 Department of Environmental Resources
- RG 044 Pennsylvania Securities Commission
- RG 045 Department of Mines and Mineral Industries
- RG 046 Valley Forge Park Commission
- RG 047 County Governments
- RG 048 Municipal Governments
- RG 049 Pennsylvania Higher Educational Facilities Authority
- RG 050 Pennsylvania Public School Employees' Retirement System
- RG 051 Department of Forestry
- RG 052 Department of Transportation
- RG 053 Department of Banking and Securities
- RG 055 School Districts
- RG 056 State Ethics Commission
- RG 057 State System of Higher Education
- RG 058 Department of Corrections
- RG 059 State Employees' Retirement System (SERS)
- RG 060 Pennsylvania Public Television Network Commission

- RG 061 Office of the Inspector General
- RG 062 Special Courts
- RG 063 Commonwealth Court
- RG 064 Office of the Lieutenant Governor
- RG 065 Department of Conservation and Natural Resources
- RG 066 Department of Environmental Protection
- RG 067 Environmental Hearing Board
- RG 069 Pennsylvania Emergency Management Agency (PEMA)
- RG 070 Office of the Attorney General
- RG 071 Department of Community and Economic Development
- RG 072 Fish and Boat Commission
- RG 073 Public Employee Retirement Commission
- RG 074 Independent Regulatory Review Commission
- RG 075 Pennsylvania Infrastructure Investment Authority (PENNVEST)
- RG 076 Department of Aging
- RG 077 State Tax Equalization Board
- RG 078 State Public School Building Authority
- RG 079 Pennsylvania Housing Finance Agency
- RG 080 MILRITE (Making Industry and Labor Right in Today's Economy) Council
- RG 081 Board of Probation and Parole
- RG 082 Gaming Control Board
- RG 083 Pennsylvania Municipal Retirement System

- RG 084 Pennsylvania Health Care Cost Containment Council
- RG 393 Affiliated Archives: Records of the Brevet Major General John Frederick Hartranft as Special Provost Marshal for the Trial and Execution of the Assassins of President Lincoln (from NARA RG 393)

The last record group, RG 393, is a National Archives collection but maintained at the Pennsylvania State Archives as a National Archives Affiliate Archives. Keeping Hartranft's records from his time as a Major General with his papers as Governor, helps researchers and makes the collection whole.

For genealogists, most of these record groups are of little interest, unless an ancestor worked in that agency or department.

The most genealogically relevant record groups are RG 11 Department of Health for vital record certificates, RG 19 Department of Military and Veterans' Affairs for military service awards, RG 33 Supreme Court of Pennsylvania and RG 38 Superior Court for naturalization records, and RG 47 County Governments and RG 48 Municipal Governments for local records.

RG 48 records are not a complete set of the 67 counties and thousands of municipalities of the state. The majority of county records remain the county where they were created. However, some original county and municipal records have landed at the Archives and remain there. Most notable in RG 48 are the records of Allegheny City, which was incorporated into the City of Pittsburgh in 1907.

The Archives also has onsite over 18,000 FamilySearch microfilm rolls containing county and municipal records, including wills, deeds, 19th-century vital records, and tax listings. These are the same records which are available to researchers at home through their FamilySearch account or at a FamilySearch Center.

Out of all the state government records, some of the most popular on-site are early land records. Most of this collection is currently not digitized and indexed for research from home. The first purchases and assignments of land ownership occurred in 1667, fifteen years before William Penn's arrival. Detailed information on all these records in RG

21 Proprietary Government, along with digital images of the indexes and other frequently used documents are on the Pennsylvania State Archives website. This collection includes:

- Purchases from William Penn
- Land warrants and applications
- Original surveys and copied survey books
- Land patent books
- Warrant registers and patent indexes
- Warrantee maps for about 30% of Pennsylvania's townships
- Donation Lands papers, noting grants to Pennsylvania Line Revolutionary War veterans
- Virginia land claims
- Connecticut claimants' files
- Land office map collection

The next most popular records for research on-site in the archives are more collections that are also not yet digitized. These include the following collections:

- State road and turnpike maps (1706–1873)
- Port of Philadelphia records (1728–1982)
- Internal improvements files (1777–1902)
- Pennsylvania Turnpike Commission records (1882–2009)
- Mine accident registers (1899–1975)
- Industrial Board minutes (1914–1986)
- Department of Highways photographs (1900–1966)
- State penitentiary records (1829–1972)

- State hospital records, known at the time as insane asylums or lunatic asylums

- Pennsylvania Supreme Court naturalizations (1794–1868)

- Pennsylvania Farm Censuses (1924 and 1927)

The non-governmental record groups, also called manuscript groups, are designated with MG. The most popular manuscript groups for researchers include:

- MG 011 Map Collection

- MG 213 Postcard Collection

- MG 218 Photograph Collection

- MG 219 Philadelphia Commercial Museum Photograph Collection

- MG 281 Samuel W. Kuhnert Papers

- MG 286 Penn Central Collection (PRR)

- Cornwall Furnace records (1757–1940)

- Line Grove Furnace records (1781–1914)

- Lehigh Coal and Navigation Company records (1792–1978)

- Pennsylvania Main Line Canal records (1816–1868)

- Fall Brook Railroad and Coal Company records (1819–1938)

- Baldwin Locomotive Works records (1834–1962)

- Pennsylvania Railroad records (1835–1968)

- Lehigh Valley Railroad records (1849–1962)

For in-depth information on these records, digital images of indexes, and frequently accessed documents, please visit the catalog on the State Archives website. Collections are described in detail there, and these are just the highlights of what is available. Additionally, collections are moving from paper to digital regularly and the catalog is the way to access those collections.

Digitized Collections

If you are a genealogist or history researcher, the most popular and frequently used records of the Pennsylvania State Archive have been digitized and are accessible from home. Ancestry has a longstanding contract with the Archives and has made all the following paper records into digital images searchable on their site:

- Birth and death registrations (1852–1854) and some later county registrations (1893–1906)[2]

- Original 20th-century birth and death certificates from 1906 to year limited by law.[3]

- Marriage records (1742–1762, and 1852–1854)

- Military service award records spanning World War 1 through the Vietnam War

- Military records of Pennsylvania citizens related to the Revolutionary War, War of 1812, War with Mexico, and Civil War

- Philadelphia ships' lists documenting German passengers (1727–1808)

- Colonial naturalization records (1740–1773)

- U.S. Direct Tax of 1798, also known as the Glass Tax

- Pennsylvania Septennial Censuses (1779–1821)

Direct links to the collections listed above are all on Ancestry's Pennsylvania family history research page: **https://www.ancestry.com/search/places/usa/pennsylvania**

The Pennsylvania Archives Book Series

The earliest records of the Pennsylvania government were transcribed and published in the *Pennsylvania Archives* book series. Unfortunately, once the transcription was completed, the originals records were destroyed. The books are no longer in print, but digital copies are available on multiple websites. Perhaps the most useful version for genealogy researchers is available for free on Fold 3 at **https://www.fold3.com/publication/450/us-pennsylvania-archives-1660-1780**.

A full summary description of what is in each volume, across the series, is found on The Pennsylvania State Archives website at **https://www.phmc.pa.gov/Archives/Research-Online/Pages/Published-PA-Archives.asp**x.

For Further Reading

There are three excellent books, available from online booksellers or in many large libraries and genealogical societies, to help understand the Pennsylvania State Archives collections in-depth.

- *Guide to Genealogical Sources at the Pennsylvania State Archives*, by Robert M. Dructor
- *Guide to the Published Pennsylvania Archives*, by the Pennsylvania Historical and Museum Commission
- *Guide to African American Resources at the Pennsylvania State Archives*, by Ruth E. Hodge
- *Pennsylvania Land Records: A History and Guide for Research*, by Donna Bingham Munger

State Library of Pennsylvania

Location: The Forum Building, 607 South Drive, Harrisburg, PA, 17126
Telephone: 717-783-5950
Email: ra-reflib@pa.gov
Website: https://www.statelibrary.pa.gov
Catalog:
https://www.statelibrary.pa.gov/GeneralPublic/Collections
Digital collections: https://powerlibrary.org
Libguides: https://pa-gov.libguides.com

History

The State Library of Pennsylvania, known as the Pennsylvania State Library until 1971, has a legacy dating back to the earliest days of the Commonwealth. The Library began on December 5, 1775, when the Pennsylvania General Assembly tasked Benjamin Franklin with procuring a copy of Statutes at Large and reference maps. The institution focused its holdings on useful documents and books for state representatives.

The State Library expanded its scope in the late 19th-century. William Henry Egle, M.D., who served as the state librarian from 1887 to 1898, played a crucial role in diversifying the library's holdings. He emphasized expanding the newspaper collection to include papers from every county, and he secured an additional, larger, library space. In February 1897, the old capitol building, housing the Pennsylvania State Library at the time, suffered a devastating fire. While materials in the new building were saved, some crucial historical and legislative documents still in the capitol were lost to the flames.

Thomas Lynch Montgomery, serving as state librarian from 1903 to 1921, significantly advanced the library's mission. He collaborated with other library organizations to enhance statewide access to materials and oversaw the diversification of the library's collection. Montgomery played a pivotal role in the creation of the Pennsylvania State Archives in 1903 and the State Museum of Pennsylvania in 1905, although these divisions were later separated from the State Library in 1941. (See the history of the Pennsylvania State Archives for details.)

Today the State Library of Pennsylvania is located in the Forum Building on the state capitol grounds. The Forum Building was closed for renovations from July 2019 through November 2023, cutting off access to the majority of the research collection.

The State Library is a part of the Pennsylvania Department of Education and sets policy and collection guidelines for all local public libraries around the Commonwealth.

The State Library of Pennsylvania is often confused with both the University of Pennsylvania in Philadelphia and Penn State University

ARCHIVES IN PENNSYLVANIA FOR GENEALOGY RESEARCH   59

in State College. These three organizations are not affiliated with each other in any way.

Collections

The State Library of Pennsylvania houses a diverse collection of materials that reflect its mission of preserving Pennsylvania's heritage and providing valuable resources to the public and state government. Some notable collections and areas of focus include:

- Pennsylvania State Documents Depository: As the official depository for printed publications of the Commonwealth of Pennsylvania, the library's collection offers a historical repository of government materials dating back to the 1700s. A system of depository libraries extends access beyond Harrisburg, with many publications available electronically.

- Federal Documents Depository: The library participates in the U.S. Government Printing Office Federal Depository Program, with a collection dating back to the mid-1800s. It serves as the Regional Federal Depository Library for the Commonwealth, receiving copies of U.S. government publications. Many of these publications are accessible electronically.

- State Law Library: This collection comprises laws, regulations, and higher court decisions of the U.S. government and all fifty states. It also includes online resources available to State Government employees.

- Genealogy and Local History: One of the library's largest services, this collection includes indexes, genealogies, state and county histories, family histories, city directories, atlases, ship passenger lists, and records of churches and cemeteries. It also offers access to Federal Census records for Pennsylvania from 1790 to 1930.

- Pennsylvania Newspapers: The communities of the Commonwealth published over 8,000 newspaper titles. There is no comprehensive list of all the newspaper titles (The Library of Congress listing is considered the best reference), but the

Library holds the largest Pennsylvania newspaper collection, available for lending through public libraries across the state and country.

Historical Society of Pennsylvania

Location: 1300 Locust Street, Philadelphia, PA 19107
Website: https://hsp.org
Email: Chat available through link on homepage
Telephone: (215) 732-6200
Card Catalog:
https://www.familysearch.org/search/collection/2524622
Online Catalog: https://discover.hsp.org

History

The Historical Society of Pennsylvania (HSP), established in 1824, is one of the largest libraries of American history in the nation, with over 21 million manuscripts, books, and graphic images. HSP holds in its vaults a draft of the U.S. Constitution, a printer's proof of the Declaration of Independence, and one of the earliest photographs created in America.

HSP serves thousands of on-site researchers each year and and hundreds through its virtual programs for paid members. In addition, HSP is a leading center for the documentation and study of ethnic communities and immigrant experiences in the 20th-century, and the largest family history library in Pennsylvania.

The Society previously had two publications: the *Pennsylvania Magazine of History and Biography* (PMHB), a scholarly journal published three times a year, and *Pennsylvania Legacies*, a semi-annual public history magazine. As of 2021, both publications have ceased, but the back issues hold genealogical and historical treasures. Digital versions of the PMHB from 1877–2021 are hosted by Penn State University Libraries at **https://journals.psu.edu/pmhb/about** and *Pennsylvania Legacies* from 2001–2020 are hosted by JSTOR at **https://www.jstor.org/journal/pennlega**.

Collections

HSP's collections cover a broad range of topics — from Pennsylvania and adjacent states, to the formation of the United States, national ethnic organizations, and the Philadelphia area itself. It generally does not collect government-owned documents, postcards, ephemera, unidentified photographs, or individual documents (although these items will be found inside of existing collections).

In addition, HSP does not add to its art and artifact collection which is now in the custody and control of the Atwater Kent Museum. HSP has a cooperative agreement with the Library Company of Philadelphia (LCP), located next door, by which LCP administers the Society's pre-1820 imprints while the Society administers LCP's manuscript collections.

Researching at HSP involves using two different catalogs. The original catalog is a library card catalog organized by collection type, then alphabetically. In 2015, FamilySearch digitized the almost 1 million individual cards in this catalog and hosts the images at **https://www.familysearch.org/search/collection/2524622**. Currently, researchers can flip through the card images to look through the catalog; it is not indexed for search through the search bar.

The second catalog for research is the Discover Catalog available on the website at **https://discover.hsp.org**. Items listed in this catalog include more recent additions to the archival collection and items more frequently researched. The Discover Catalog is not a comprehensive listing of what is at HSP. Creating a free account in the Discover Catalog allows the saving of items in list form to take for in-person research. Any relevant finding aids for items are also linked through the Discover Catalog.

The Society began digitizing items in 2020 and making them freely available on its website at **https://digitallibrary.hsp.org/index.php**. One unique item of interest to researchers of enslaved peoples and their enslavers is the "Census of the Condition of Colored People in Philadelphia, 1847." This detailed listing of every black resident of Philadelphia is a genealogical treasure. Images of the census are at **https://digitallibrary.hsp.org/index.php/Detail/objects/21**.

Floor Plan of the Research Rooms

On-site research is conducted in the rooms on the first floor of the building. This floorplan shows the different research rooms:

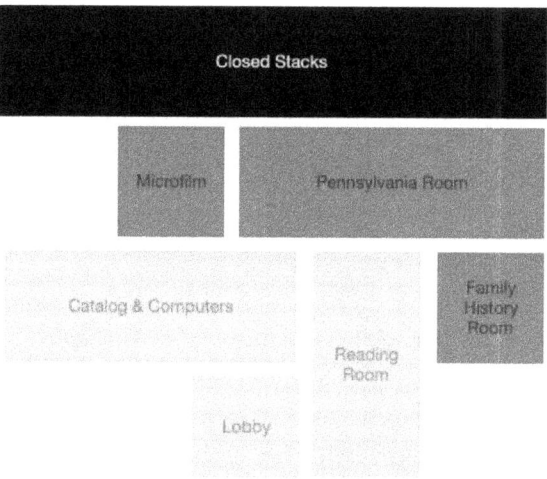

HSP floor plan, created by Denyse Allen.

- The Reading Room is full of large communal tables behind a railing. This is where requests for items in the Closed Stacks are made and where those items are read, then returned.

- The Pennsylvania Room contains shelves of transcribed records and published histories from all 67 counties. The collection known as "The Greens and the Browns" of church records is also here. See the details of that collection under the Genealogical Society of Pennsylvania listing below.

- The Family History Room contains published genealogies. These have been selected for their relevance to Pennsylvania and professional presentation of the information.

- The Microfilm Room is self-service for research of newspapers and church records.

A small lunch area with seating next to the lobby is available to researchers for breaks throughout the day. Researchers also have access to lockers to hold their personal effects not permitted in the research areas.

Appointments are required for research. Research appointments are free for members and $10 per day for non-members. Staff will cover all research rules the day of on-site research. There are no photocopiers available, but researchers can take digital images of items for no charge.

Genealogical Society of Pennsylvania

Location: 2100 Byberry Road, Suite 111, Philadelphia PA 19116
Telephone: 267-686-2296
Email: Info@genpa.org
Website: https://genpa.org
Catalog: https://genpa.org/gsp-collections

History

The Genealogical Society of Pennsylvania (GSP) is a non-profit organization based in Philadelphia. Founded in 1892 as part of the Historical Society of Pennsylvania, GSP was one of the first genealogical societies in the United States. Their mission is to provide support to promote genealogical research through education, preservation, and access to Pennsylvania-related genealogical information.[4] While GSP is not technically an archive, the organization has collected and continues to preserve historical records of genealogical interest.

In the past, the Society had two publications: The *Penn in Hand* newsletter and *The Pennsylvania Genealogical Magazine*. *Penn in Hand* was published from 1980 to 2007 and 2011 to 2016. The newsletter focused on news of of the Society, genealogical events, and updates from county genealogical societies around the state. Some past issues are digitally available on the GSP website, but issues from 1980 to 1999 are in original form in the GSP Library.

The *Pennsylvania Genealogical Magazine* (PGM) was also called called the *Publications of the Genealogical Society of Pennsylvania*. Issues were published from 1895 until 2015, spanning 120 years . Articles featured indexed records, historical background of immigration and ethnic groups, research methodologies, and published genealogies. Some issues are digitally available through the GSP website, but all past issues in original form are housed at GSP.

Collections

The first collections created by GSP were of church registers, funeral home and cemetery records, and photocopies of family Bible pages. The emphasis of these collections appears to be on proving patriotic lineage to the American Revolution.

Each set of records was bound in dark green or brown covers when it was made, so the collection is fondly called "The Greens and the Browns." GSP housed these collections at HSP for ease of access for researchers. The entire set of books was digitized by Ancestry in 2012 and is found in the compilation "Pennsylvania and New Jersey, U.S., Church and Town Records" at **https://www.ancestry.com/search/collections/2451**. (Ancestry added more records than just this GSP collection to their digital collection.) A full listing of the names and locations of the churches and cemeteries in "The Greens and the Browns" collection are found in this twenty-four page PDF document at **https://hsp.org/sites/default/files/hsp_film_collection_on_ancestry.pdf** .

Today, the GSP Library holds published genealogies, town and county histories, and periodicals at its Byberry Road office. The Library items are listed in the "GSP Library Catalog" on the GSP website. Genealogical collections are available on the website in either the "Member Resources" or "Public Resources" areas. There are some original manuscript collections at GSP, but these are not cataloged or available for research. GSP accepts donations of genealogical collections from researchers. Additionally, GSP acts as a FamilySearch Affiliate Library, providing access to digital collections that have restrictions on FamilySearch.

National Archives and Record Administration, Philadelphia Branch

Location: 14700 Townsend Road, Philadelphia, PA 19154
Telephone: 215-305-2044
Email: Philadelphia.archives@nara.gov
Website: https://www.archives.gov/philadelphia
Catalog: https://www.archives.gov/philadelphia/holdings
Digital collections:
https://www.archives.gov/philadelphia/digitized-genealogical-records

History

The National Archives and Records Administration (NARA) was created in 1934 to protect the historical records of the federal government. Prior to 1934, records were held in various places with no security or special care for storage conditions. The original National Archives Building on the Mall in Washington, DC was opened in 1935. Today, NARA operates more than 40 facilities with over 1,100 federal employees nationwide. The mission of NARA is to provide public access to government records in order to strengthen democracy by allowing citizens to understand their history, hold their government accountable, and participate more effectively in their government.[5]

The National Archives at Philadelphia was also known as the National Archives, Mid-Atlantic Region for a period of time. Its focus is federal government records from Pennsylvania, New Jersey, Delaware, Virginia, and Maryland. The first location of the National Archives in Philadelphia was 900 Market Street in Center City. It is now located in a warehouse on Townsend Road, in the Northeast section of Philadelphia. The move was due to the lack of storage space.

Collections

The collections of all National Archives locations, including Presidential Libraries, are contained in The National Archives Catalog. The National Archives Catalog stores descriptions of the NARA's nationwide holdings, organized by record group, then by series, file units. Item descriptions link to digital images if there is one. It is important to note that individual names are not typically included in the item descriptions, but records may still contain information about individuals.

Many people find the Catalog overwhelming to use. One helpful substitute is the three volume Guide to Federal Records in the National Archives of the United States. It is no longer in print, but used copies can be found through book sellers online. A transcription is also on The National Archives website at **https://www.archives.gov/research/guide-fed-records** .

To search for archival collections housed at National Archives in Philadelphia on the Catalog, use the "advanced" settings or the left-most column on any page to limit searches to "National Archives at Philadelphia." To view a simplified summary list of collections visit the Philadelphia website at **https://www.archives.gov/philadelphia/holdings** .

The most popular holdings at The National Archives at Philadelphia for genealogists include:

- Naturalization records processed through federal courts.

- Ship's passenger lists for arrivals at the ports of Philadelphia and Baltimore.

- Nonpopulation census records, including agricultural, mortality, and manufacturing schedules.

Many of these popular collections are digitized, or in the process of being digitized, by Ancestry and FamilySearch, both NARA Digitization Partners. To stay informed as to which record sets are available digitally and access the links to where they are, view the continually updated list "Microfilm Publications and Original Records Digitized by Our Digitization Partners" on NARA's website at **https://www.archives.gov/digitization/digitized-by-partners**. Selected finding aids, including the useful *Guide to Archival Holdings at the National Archives at Philadelphia,* are available on the National Archives at Philadelphia website at **https://www.archives.gov/philadelphia/holdings** . Another helpful resource is the out-of-print booklet, *Guide to Records in the National Archives Mid-Atlantic Region.* This booklet explains what is found locally versus in Washington D.C. It is found on FamilySearch at **https://www.familysearch.org/library/books/records/item/216799-guide-to-records-in-the-national-archives-mid-atlantic-region**.

It is important to note that researchers of Pennsylvania citizens, will need to use the National Archives in Washington D.C. and other branches of the National Archives depending on the focus of the research. Federal records are organized by their federal branch or department location, not by the location of the individuals in the records.

FamilySearch Affiliate Libraries and FamilySearch Centers

Locations: https://www.familysearch.org/centers/locations

The Utah Genealogical Society, now known as FamilySearch, microfilmed records in courthouses, churches, and other organizations all over the United States in the mid-20th century. These microfilms are now digitized on FamilySearch's website as both indexed, searchable images and browsable images. The majority of these records are viewable from home with a free FamilySearch account. Some of the records have restricted access and are viewable only at at a FamilySearch Center or Affiliate Library. Any restrictions on records were requested by the original record holders.

FamilySearch Centers are located within The Church of Jesus Christ of Latter-day Saints' churches. The Centers provide access to all the restricted collections as well as free access to Ancestry. FamilySearch Affiliate Libraries are public libraries or organizations which have contracted with FamilySearch to provide access to restricted records.

You do not need to be in Pennsylvania to research in Pennsylvania records on FamilySearch. As long as you can access the internet, a FamilySearch Center, or an Affiliate Library, you can search through the millions of records available.

1. The Pennsylvania State Archives homepage, (https://www.phmc.pa.gov/Archives/Pages/default.aspx)

2. For more information on vital records from Pennsylvania's colonial beginning to present day, see my book *Pennsylvania Vital Records Research*.

3. Pennsylvania law allows public access of original birth certificates 105 years after birth and death certificates 50 years after death.

4. "About GSP," *Genealogical Society of Pennsylvania* (https://genpa.org/about-gsp/).

5. The mission of NARA has been revised a few times in the past three years. The current version is found at: "Mission, Vision and Values," *National Archives* (https://www.archives.gov/about/info/mission).

Chapter 6

Regional Pennsylvania Archives

THE TERM "REGIONAL ARCHIVES" is not one these institutions use to describe themselves. It is a term invented to describe archives that focus their collections across a region of several counties, but less than the whole state. The main regional archives in Pennsylvania focus on three different geographies: the Philadelphia area, Central Pennsylvania, and Western Pennsylvania.

These regionally focused archives all employ professional archivists for processing. Their catalogs are all online and searchable from anywhere, and include detailed listings of collection contents. Finding aids are also common in these archives and usually downloadable as PDF files for easy reference by researchers.

For each archive in this chapter there is a short history, links to its website, catalog and/or finding aids, and the highlights of the collection for genealogists. Each of these archives requests researchers contact them prior to arrival for consultation. Email is the preferred communication method. When you email, state your planned dates for research and collections you would like to review. As of the date of publication, there is no fee for researching in any of these locations.

Also included in this section is the Philadelphia Area Consortium of Special Collections Libraries (PACSCL). PACSCL is not an archive, but an association of archives located in and around Philadelphia. It is an incredibly helpful organization for research.

These are all "must do" archives for researchers. Their collections are updated often, and the range of their materials ensures one of them will have something to meet your research goals.

***

Penn State University, Eberly Family Special Collections Library

Location: 104 Paterno Library, University Park, PA 16802
Telephone: (814)865-1793
Email: spcollections@psu.edu
Website: https://libraries.psu.edu/specialcollections
Catalog: https://catalog.libraries.psu.edu
Finding Aids:
https://aspace.libraries.psu.edu/repositories/resources
Images of the Collections:
https://www.flickr.com/photos/pennstatespecial/albums

History

Penn State University, formally named The Pennsylvania State University, was founded in 1855 in Centre County. Penn State began as a land-grant college with an emphasis on applying scientific principles to agriculture. The college's curriculum expanded in the 1890s to include other sciences, engineering, and liberal arts.

In the 1930s, Penn State established branch campuses across the state, culminating in the twenty-four Penn State campuses we have today. Each branch campus, also called a commonwealth campus, has its own library, and some have archival collections. Savvy researchers working on topics outside of central Pennsylvania will be sure to check the collections of the Penn State Libraries at the campus closest to their research subject. A listing of all campuses in Chapter 8: Archives and Special Collections at Colleges and Universities.

From its beginning, the college library at Penn State's Main Campus in State College collected archival materials, segmenting them into their "special collections." The name of the Eberly Special Collections Library comes from Ralph Dorn Hetzel and Grace Milham Eberly, whose financial contributions expanded its holdings. This archive focuses on collecting materials related to the history of Pennsylvania in general, and the lives of people in central counties of Pennsylvania in particular.

Highlights of the Collections

Below are some popular collections for genealogy research. Be sure to check the catalog and finding aids for additional collections relevant to your particular research.

- Amalgamated Association of Iron, Steel, and Tin Workers of North America records
  https://libraries.psu.edu/about/collections/amalgamated-association-iron-steel-and-tin-workers-north-america-records

- Civil War diaries
  https://libraries.psu.edu/about/collections/civil-war-era-diaries

- Pennsylvania Center for Folklore Collection
  https://libraries.psu.edu/about/collections/pennsylvania-center-folklore-collection

- Collection of business and financial books from Central Pennsylvania
  https://arks.libraries.psu.edu/ark:/42409/fa8wc9q

The following digital collections are images of original records at the Eberly Special Collections Library:

- German-Language Broadsides in North America, 1730–1830
  https://libraries.psu.edu/about/collections/german-language-broadsides-north-america-1730-1830

- Pennsylvania German Broadsides and Fraktur Collection

https://libraries.psu.edu/about/collections/pennsylvania-german-broadsides-and-fraktur

- Non-Reporting Drafted Men and Deserters of the Union Army
https://libraries.psu.edu/about/collections/non-reporting-drafted-men-and-deserters

- The People's Contest, A Civil War Era Digital Archiving Project: Diaries, journals, and photographs from various participants in the Civil War. Also features a searchable database of Union Army Deserters.
https://peoplescontest.psu.edu/digital-collections

Heinz History Center, Detre Library and Archives

Location: 1212 Smallman Street, Pittsburgh, PA 15222
Telephone: (412)454-6364
Email: library@heinzhistorycenter.org
Website:
https://www.heinzhistorycenter.org/research/detre-library-archives
Catalog: https://s92015.eos-intl.net/S92015/OPAC/Index.aspx
Finding aids: https://historicpittsburgh.org/findingaids
Digital collections: https://historicpittsburgh.org

Background

The Detre Library and Archives is located in the Heinz History Center which opened in 1996. The Heinz History Center is named for Senator John H. Heinz, heir to the H.J. Heinz Company and U.S. Senator, who died in a plane crash in April 1991. The Archives is named after Dr. Thomas Detre, a Pittsburgh neurologist and philanthropist, and his wife, Katherine, who contributed the founding resources.

The Heinz History Center is the new name for the Historical Society of Western Pennsylvania (HSWP). HSWP was founded in 1879 by a group of Pittsburgh business and political leaders focused on preserving the history of Pittsburgh and its surrounding counties. The first materials in the Detre Library and Archives were from the archives of HSWP.

The first home of the HSWP archives was the Carnegie Library of Pittsburgh, Oakland branch, beginning in 1893. The archives remained there for almost 100 years until the move to the sixth floor of the Heinz History Center. HSWP has published the *Journal of Western Pennsylvania History* since 1918. A searchable archive of all issues more than one year old is hosted by Penn State University at **https://journals.psu.edu/wph/index** Issues feature "treasures" from the Detre Library and Archives providing an in-depth look at a variety of collections.

Today the Detre Library and Archives' collection contains almost 1 million archival items focused on the counties of western Pennsylvania: Allegheny, Armstrong, Beaver, Bedford, Butler, Cambria, Clarion, Clearfield, Crawford, Elk, Fayette, Forest, Greene, Indiana, Jefferson, Lawrence, Mercer, Somerset, Venango, Washington, and Westmoreland. There are over 1,500 finding aids describing the Library and Archives' largest collections. These finding aids are well-organized and easy-to-understand for new researchers. They are found on the Historic Pittsburgh website, and in the Detre Library and Archives catalog.

The Detre Library and Archives has strong relationships with other Pittsburgh archival institutions. Their partnership with the University of Pittsburgh allowed for digitization of useful and popular archival materials in its collection. These are hosted on the website *Historic Pittsburgh* at **https://historicpittsburgh.org**.

The research room is a spacious 12,000 square feet with a dozen large tables, comfortable chairs, and good lighting. Lockers are available to hold personal belongings for the day. Parking is across the street and paid on an hourly or daily rate.

Highlights of the Collections

- ALCOA Oral Histories: Collected from 1989–1999, these cassettes and transcripts feature employees on the manufacturing of aluminum products in the 1970s and 1980s.

- Family Papers: Early 20th-century Pittsburgh was flooded with wealth from manufacturing. Many prominent citizens photographs, letters, diaries, and business records are preserved here. Search by family name, time period, and company name.

- H.J. Heinz Company: Photographs of employees, products, and manufacturing of the famous ketchup and pickles. Also company and employee records and correspondence.

- Pittsburgh Floods: Photographs and news clippings of damage from the Ohio, Allegheny, and Monongahela Rivers flooding over the decades.

- Pittsburgh Public Schools: Correspondence, photographs, reports, scrapbooks, and business records from 90 schools.

- Postcard Collection: Images of early 20th-century Pittsburgh, but also a few of other Pennsylvania counties.

- Religious Records: Dozens of congregational records of various faiths are housed here. Use the catalog to search for locations and names of the churches and synagogues.

- Writt-Richards Family Papers and Photographs: Featuring the lives of African American families who moved to Pittsburgh the early 20th-century and became part of the middle class.

- The Jewish Encyclopedia of Western Pennsylvania: the history of synagogues, businesses, and organizations as early as 1755 for the western half of the state, including Pittsburgh.

The following digital collections are hosted on *Historic Pittsburgh* at **https://historicpittsburgh.org/collections/A%2A**:

- City Directories: This digital collection is combined from Detre, Carnegie Libraries, University of Pittsburgh, and the Pittsburgh History and Landmarks Foundation. Over one hundred city and business directories from 1815–1945 at **https://historicpittsburgh.org/collection/historic-pittsburgh-city-directories**

- Hopkins Maps: The digital assortment includes Hopkins atlas style maps from 1872–1940, topographic and flood maps of Pittsburgh, warrantee maps of the first land purchases, and early 18th-century maps. All digitized on Historic Pittsburgh at **https://historicpittsburgh.org/pittsburgh-maps**.

- Manumission Papers (1792–1857): The indentures and enslavement of African Americans were filed at each county courthouse. Many have been lost over the years, but the Allegheny County records were digitized by University of Pittsburgh at **http://exhibit.library.pitt.edu/freeatlast/papers_listing.html**.

Temple University Libraries, Special Collections Research Center

Location: Charles Library, 1900 North 13th Street, Philadelphia, PA 19122
Telephone: (215)204-8257
Email: scrc@temple.edu
Website: https://library.temple.edu/scrc
Catalog: https://librarysearch.temple.edu/catalog
Finding Aids: https://library.temple.edu/finding-aids

Background

Temple University was founded in 1884 by Dr. Russell Conwell, an ordained Baptist minister and veteran of the Union Army. Conwell came to Philadelphia in 1882 to lead Grace Baptist Church in North Philadelphia and tutored classes for his factory-working congregation at night. The classes were held in the basement of the church and the students were nick-named "night owls." The owl is the school mascot today.

The Temple archival collection began in the 1890s and was housed as a "special collection" in the university library. In 1965, the university became a state-affiliated school providing it with more funding and resources. This state funding was needed to support it as the population of Philadelphia fell by 40% from 1950 to 1970. The Temple University

Library already had archival materials about the college itself, but it was this new funding that expanded the archival focus.

Temple University's Special Collections includes the Urban Archives, established in 1967, dedicated to preserving and documenting the history of the Philadelphia metropolitan area, with a particular focus on urban life, development, and culture. Researchers interested in urban planning, neighborhood development, civil rights, immigration, and the various industries once a part of the city, will find interesting archival materials here.

In 2019, Temple opened the spacious Charles Library and the Special Collections Research Center (SCRC). The new facility offers spacious areas for researchers to examine archival collections. The Charles Library is open to the public and researchers can access the SCRC through appointments.

Highlights of the Collections

The holdings at the SCRC feature the following collections:

- Blockson General and Special Collections: Publications and archival materials on Afro-American history

- Contemporary Culture Collections: Materials on social, political, and cultural movements from the 1960s to present day.

- Manuscripts and Archives Collections: The catch-all category for family papers and organizational records that do not fit in the other categories.

- Philadelphia Jewish Archives Collection: Personal papers and organizational records from in and around Philadelphia

- Printing, Publishing, and Bookselling Collections: Archival materials from book publishing companies in the city, as well as the book making process.

- Urban Archives: Collections featuring the economic, social, political, and physical development of the Philadelphia area from the 19th to 21st-centuries.

- Walter Massey Phillips Oral Histories: Over 150 interviews completed by Mr. Phillips between 1974 and 1980 about Philadelphia city government and events through the 1930s to 1970s.

- Feinstein Center Oral Histories: Interviews conducted in 2001 with fifty significant Philadelphia Jewish men and women.

- African American Migration to Philadelphia Oral Histories: Interviews recorded between 1987 and 1988 of 269 individuals who moved to Philadelphia from southern states beginning in 1916.

- George D. McDowell *Philadelphia Evening Bulletin* Photographs: A selection of photographs from the *Evening Bulletin* newspaper. Not every image from the entire run of the newspaper has been digitized, but the newspaper is microfilmed and available for research at Temple.

- John W. Mosley Photographs: Documentation of African American life in Philadelphia from the 1930s to 1960s.

- Housing Association of the Delaware Valley Photographs: Images made between 1897 and 1972 showing the living conditions of working class Philadelphians. Labeled by street address for easy searching.

Some finding aids for the SCRC collections are featured on the Temple University Libraries website. These large collections may be of interest to genealogical researchers:

- Gray Panthers, founded as the Consultation of Older and Younger Adults, organizational records (1953–2015)

- International Ladies Garment Workers Union, Philadelphia records (1829–1976)

- Jewish benevolent societies membership records (1864–2015)

- Jewish Y's and Centers of Greater Philadelphia records (1891–1969)

- Synagogue records from Adath Shalom, Beth Am Israel, and Society Hill (1921–2020)

- Roman Catholic church records from St. Peter Claver (1965–2009)

- NAACP, Philadelphia records (1943–2016)

- African American organizational records from Germantown Settlement, Black Coalition, Urban Affairs Partnership, and more (1920–1975)

- Young Women's Christian Association of Philadelphia, five different club records (1785–1982)

The finding aids on the website are only a portion of the entire holdings at the SCRC. Researchers are encouraged to email or call if they are searching for a specific type of collection for an organization, business, social movement, congregation, school, or set of family or personal papers.

The SRSC's online exhibition *The Politics of Yellow Fever in Alexander Hamilton's America: The Yellow Fever Epidemic of 1793 in Philadelphia* is helpful for researchers with ancestors in the colonial city. The 1793 Yellow Fever epidemic was the most deadly disease outbreak of colonial America. Located at: **https://sites.google.com/temple.edu/yellowfever**.

Philadelphia Area Consortium of Special Collections Libraries (PACSCL)

Website: https://pacscl.org
Members' Listing:
https://pacscl.org/who-we-are/member-libraries
Catalog: https://findingaids.library.upenn.edu

The Philadelphia Area Consortium of Special Collections Libraries (PACSCL) is not an archive, but an association of archives located in and around Philadelphia. Founded in 1985 with 16 institutions, it has grown to 35 institutions today. PACSCL members develop projects and programs to benefit researchers of all interests.

PACSCL members renew their membership in the association each year. This is the current list of members:

- The Academy of Natural Sciences, Ewell Stewart Sale Library
- The Athenaeum of Philadelphia
- Barnes Foundation
- Bryn Mawr College, Canaday Library
- City of Philadelphia Department of Records, City Archives
- The College of Physicians of Philadelphia, Historical Medical Library
- Curtis Institute of Music, John de Lancie Library and Curtis Archives
- Drexel University, Archives and Special Collections
- Free Library of Philadelphia, Special Collections Division
- German Society of Pennsylvania, Joseph P. Horner Memorial Library
- Haverford College, Quaker & Special Collections
- Independence Seaport Museum, J. Welles Henderson Research Center
- Institute for Advanced Study, Shelby White and Leon Levy Archives Center
- LaSalle University, Connelly Library
- Laurel Hill Cemetery
- Lehigh University, Linderman Library
- The Library Company of Philadelphia

- The Pennsylvania Horticultural Society, McLean Library
- Philadelphia College of Osteopathic Medicine
- Philadelphia Museum of Art, Library and Archives
- Princeton University Libraries, Special Collections
- The Rosenbach Museum and Library
- Rowan University, Libraries Archives and Special Collections
- Science History Institute, Othmer Library
- State Library of Pennsylvania
- Swarthmore College Special Collections
- Temple University Libraries, Special Collections Research Center
- Thomas Jefferson University, East Falls Archives and Special Collections
- Union League, Legacy Foundation
- United Lutheran Seminary
- University of Pennsylvania, Kislak Center for Special Collections, Rare Books, and Manuscripts
- Villanova University, Falvey Memorial Library
- Wagner Free Institute
- Widener University, Wolfgram Memorial Library
- The John J. Wilcox Jr Archive of the William Way LGBT Community Center

To learn more about each member archive, refer to its listing in Chapter 8: Archives and Special Collections at Colleges and Universities, or Chapter 9: Local Organizational, Historical, and Genealogical Archives.

One PACSCL resource that genealogists will want to use is the Philadelphia Area Archives Catalog at **https://findingaids.library.upenn.edu**. This catalog is a collection of finding aids for the most frequently researched materials across PACSCL member archives. Unfortunately, the catalog is not a comprehensive listing of every item across all member archives, so researchers will still need to look in each individual archive's catalog.

Chapter 7

County Courthouses and Archives

PENNSYLVANIA HAS 67 COUNTIES, each with its own county courthouse. When these counties were founded in the 17th through 19th centuries, a singular courthouse building was all that was needed to process and store records for county residents.

In the last couple of decades, the more populous counties established additional buildings, such as administrative centers, annexes, and archives to handle the enormous amount of paperwork and permanent county records.

County Offices and Duties

Traditionally, each county has the following offices and duties:

- **Recorder of Deeds:** Maintains copies of property deed sale transfers.

- **Register of Wills:** Processes marriage license applications and probates estates after death for those with assets over a specific dollar threshold who also have a last will and testament.

- **Orphans Court:** Probates estates after death of any size or for those without a last will and testament. Also processed marriage license applications for a period of time.

- **Prothonotary:** Administers civil court cases such as child adoption, divorce, name changes, naturalizations (prior to 1941), and other civil matters.

- **Clerk of Courts:** Administers criminal court cases.

- **Treasurer:** Maintains tax records of county residents.

- **Sheriff:** Manages county prison, maintains records of prisoners, and evicts people from land for non-payment of taxes.

- **Coroner:** Investigates suspicious and accidental deaths in the county.

Knowing the county offices and duties is important, because genealogists will usually find historical records labeled and categorized by these offices.

However, today, some of the less populous counties combined the above offices and functions. For example, in Clearfield County the new office is "Register and Recorder" combining the functions of the Recorder of Deeds and Register of Wills.

At the same time, Pennsylvania's most densely populated counties, Allegheny, and the City of Philadelphia, were permitted under state law to rename the above offices entirely. In Allegheny County there is a "Real Estate" office which performs the function of the Recorder of Deeds, and there is a "Department of Court Records" which functions as the Register of Wills, Orphans Court, Prothonotary, and Clerk of Courts combined. In Philadelphia there is a "Department of Revenue" instead of Treasurer, and a separate "Marriage License Department" to process and store all the marriage license applications within the Register of Wills.

Despite this renaming and combining of functions today, the core list of county offices and functions listed above will help genealogists search records of the 17th through 20th centuries.

How to Start Researching in County Records

The key to county courthouse research is to be clear about the type of record you are searching for and the approximate year it was created.

If the county has its own archive for county government records, most records created prior to 1990 will be stored there. If a county has a separate archive location, it is listed below. If the county does not have an archive, then the records are almost always still in the courthouse (or adjacent administrative building).

Some counties have also transferred their oldest records to local historical societies to make them accessible for research. Given the speed with which things change, it is a best practice to contact the county courthouse prior to any in-person research to confirm where the records are.

County Records Available Online

It also should be noted that FamilySearch microfilmed county records in every county courthouse in Pennsylvania in the 1950s through 1970s. These microfilms are now all digitized and browsable on FamilySearch.org in the Catalog section of the website. Enter the county name and 'Pennsylvania' in the location field to see the listing of what is available.

Artificial Intelligence (AI) tools are being used to read these images and create searchable databases. This means that soon every county record should be as easily searchable as census records. This is great news for researchers with difficulty navigating the old courthouse indexes. You will be able to access these in the FamilySearch Catalog, and also through the main search function on FamilySearch.

It is important to note that when these records were microfilmed, not every record in the courthouse in every county was preserved. For example, tax records were often missed, but they do exist at the courthouse. Sometimes naturalization records were not filmed, but they also are still archived at the courthouse. And the one record genealogists want to be sure to obtain is full probate files. These files were rarely microfilmed by FamilySearch, but they are still preserved by the county courthouse and waiting for researchers.

In short, if it is not online, contact the county courthouse listed below and request copies of the records you need.

Look on PA Ancestors.com for more details on all the county records and how to use them to further your research.

Tip: To find if a county has any information online for genealogists, type "genealogy" in the search box on the county's website. Genealogists are the most frequent researchers in courthouses and many counties provide up-to-date information for them.

***

Adams County

County of Adams
117 Baltimore Street
Gettysburg, PA 17325
Phone: (717)334-6781
Website: https://www.adamscountypa.gov

***

Allegheny County

Allegheny County Office Building
542 Forbes Avenue
Pittsburgh, PA 15219
Phone: (412)350-4636
Website: https://www.alleghenycounty.us

***

Armstrong County

Armstrong County Courthouse
500 E. Market Street, Suite 102
Kittanning, PA 16201
Phone: (724)548-3236
Website: http://www.co.armstrong.pa.us

***

BEAVER COUNTY

Beaver County Courthouse
810 Third Street
Beaver, PA 15009
Phone: (724)728-5700
Website: https://www.beavercountypa.gov

***

BEDFORD COUNTY

Bedford County Courthouse
200 South Juliana Street
Bedford, PA 15522
Phone: (724)728-5700
Website: https://www.bedfordcountypa.org

***

BERKS COUNTY

Berks County Courthouse
633 Court Street
Reading, PA 19601
Phone: (610) 478-6970
Website: https://www.countyofberks.com

***

BLAIR COUNTY

Blair County Courthouse
423 Allegheny Street
Hollidaysburg, PA 16648
Phone: (814) 693-3000
Website: https://www.blairco.org

***

BRADFORD COUNTY

Bradford County Courthouse
301 Main Street
Towanda, PA 18848
Phone: (570) 265-1727
Website: https://bradfordcountypa.org

***

BUCKS COUNTY

Bucks County Courthouse Archive Center, 3rd Floor
55 East State Street
Doylestown, PA 18901
Phone: (215)348-6000
Website: https://www.buckscounty.gov

***

Butler County

Butler County Government Center
124 West Diamond Street
Butler, PA 16003
Phone: (724) 284-1409
Website: https://www.butlercountypa.gov

***

Cambria County

Cambria County Courthouse
200 South Center Street
Ebensburg, PA 15931
Phone: (814) 472-5440
Website: https://www.cambriacountypa.gov

***

Cameron County

Cameron County Courthouse
20 East Fifth Street
Emporium, PA 15834
Phone: (814) 486-3349
Website: https://www.cameroncountypa.com

***

Carbon County

Carbon County Administration Building
2 Hazard Square
Jim Thorpe, PA 18229
Phone: (570) 325-2651
Website: https://www.carboncountypa.gov

***

Centre County

Willowbank County Office Building
414 Homes Street, Suite #2
Bellefonte, PA 16823
Phone: (814) 355-6724
Website: https://www.centrecountypa.gov

***

Chester County

Chester County Administration Archives and Records
601 Westtown Road, Suite 080
West Chester, PA 19380
Phone: (610) 344-6760
Website: https://www.chesco.org/192/Archives-Records

Chester County Courthouse
313 West Market Street
West Chester, PA 19380
Phone: (610) 334-6330
Website: https://www.chesco.org

***

CLARION COUNTY

Clarion County Administration Office
330 Main Street
Clarion, PA 16214
Phone: (814) 226-4000
Website: https://www.co.clarion.pa.us

***

CLEARFIELD COUNTY

Clearfield County Courthouse
1 North Second Street
Clearfield, PA 16830
Phone: (814) 765-2641
Website: https://clearfieldco.org

***

CLINTON COUNTY

Clinton County Courthouse
2 Piper Way
Lock Haven, PA 17745
Phone: (570) 893-4010
Website: https://www.clintoncountypa.gov

***

COLUMBIA COUNTY

Columbia County Courthouse
35 West Main Street
Bloomsburg, PA 17815
Phone: (570) 389-5614
Website: http://www.columbiapa.org

***

CRAWFORD COUNTY

Crawford County Courthouse
903 Diamond Park
Meadville, PA 16355
Phone: (814) 373-2537
Website: https://www.crawfordcountypa.net

***

Cumberland County

County of Cumberland
1 Courthouse Square
Carlisle, PA 17013
Phone: (717) 240-6100
Website: https://www.cumberlandcountypa.gov

***

Dauphin County

Dauphin County Courthouse
101 Market Street
Harrisburg, PA 17101
Phone: (717) 780-6500
Website: https://www.dauphincounty.gov

***

Delaware County

Archives of Delaware County
340 North Middletown Road, Building 19
Lima, PA 19063
Phone: (610) 891-5620
Website:
https://delconew.azurewebsites.net/departments/archives.html

Delaware County Government Center Complex
201 West Front Street
Media, PA 19063
Phone: (610) 891-4000
Website: https://www.delcopa.gov

***

Elk County

Elk County Courthouse
240 Main Street
Ridgeway, PA 15853
Phone: (814) 776-5349
Website: http://www.co.elk.pa.us

***

Erie County

Erie County Courthouse
140 West Sixth Street
Erie, PA 16501
Phone: (814) 451-6237
Website: https://www.eriecountypa.gov

***

Fayette County

Fayette County Courthouse
61 East Main Street
Uniontown, PA 15401
Phone: (724) 430-1238
Website: https://www.fayettecountypa.org

***

Forest County

Forest County Courthouse
240 Main Street
Tionesta, PA 16353
Phone: (814) 755-3537
Website: https://www.co.forest.pa.us

***

Franklin County

Franklin County Archives Annex
625 Franklin Farms Lane
Chambersburg, PA 17202
Phone: (717) 261-3154
Website:
https://franklincountypa.gov/index.php?section=government-archives

Franklin County Courthouse
340 North Second Street
Chambersburg, PA 17202
Phone: (717) 264-4125
Website: https://www.franklincountypa.gov

***

FULTON COUNTY

Fulton County Courthouse
201 North Second Street
McConnellsburg, PA 17233
Phone: (814) 755-3537
Website: https://www.co.fulton.pa.us

***

GREENE COUNTY

Greene County Courthouse
93 East High Street
Waynesburg, PA 15370
Phone: (724) 852-5399
Website: https://www.co.greene.pa.us

***

Huntingdon County

Huntingdon County Courthouse
223 Penn Street
Huntingdon, PA 16652
Phone: (814) 643-2740
Website: https://huntingdoncountycourt.net

***

Indiana County

Indiana County Court Administration
825 Philadelphia Street
Indiana, PA 15701
Phone: (724) 465-3805
Website: https://www.indianacountypa.gov

***

Jefferson County

Jefferson County Courthouse
200 Main Street
Brookville, PA 15825
Phone: (814) 849-1610
Website: https://www.jeffersoncountypa.com

***

Juniata County

Juniata County Courthouse
Bridge & Main Streets, P.O. Box 68
Mifflintown, PA 17059
Phone: (724) 465-3805
Website:https://www.juniataco.org

***

Lackawanna County

Lackawanna County Government Center
123 Wyoming Ave
Scranton, PA 18503
Phone: (570) 963-6702
Website: https://www.lackawannacounty.org

***

Lancaster County

Lancaster County Archives
150 North Queen Street, Suite 10
Lancaster, PA 17603
Phone: (717) 299-8319
Website: https://co.lancaster.pa.us/127/Archives-Division

Lancaster County Government Center
150 North Queen Street
Lancaster, PA 17603
Phone: (717) 299-8000
Website: https://co.lancaster.pa.us

***

Lawrence County

Lawrence County Government Center
430 Court Street
New Castle, PA 16101
Phone: (724) 658-2541
Website: https://lawrencecountypa.gov

***

Lebanon County

Lebanon County Courthouse
400 South 8th Street
Lebanon, PA 17042
Phone: (717) 274-8094
Website: https://lebanoncountypa.gov

***

Lehigh County

Lehigh County Courthouse
455 Hamilton Street
Allentown, PA 18101
Phone: (610) 782-3000
Website: https://www.lehighcounty.org

***

Luzerne County

Luzerne County Courthouse
200 North River Street
Wilkes-Barre, PA 18711
Phone: (570)825-1641
Website: https://www.luzernecounty.org

***

Lycoming County

Lycoming County Courthouse
48 West Third Street
Williamsport, PA 17701
Phone: (570) 327-2251
Website: https://www.lyco.org

***

McKean County

McKean County Courthouse
500 West Main Street
Smethport, PA 16749
Phone: (814) 887-3260
Website: https://www.mckeancountypa.gov

***

Mercer County

County of Mercer
138 South Diamond Street
Mercer, PA 16137
Phone: (724) 662-3800
Website: https://www.mercercountypa.gov

***

Mifflin County

County of Mifflin
20 North Wayne Street
Lewistown, PA 17044
Phone: (717) 248-6733
Website: https://mifflinco.org

***

MONROE COUNTY

Monroe County Archive
One Quaker Plaza
Stroudsburg, PA 18360
Phone: (570) 517-3400
Website:
https://www.monroecountypa.gov/departments/archives

***

MONTGOMERY COUNTY

Montgomery County Archive
86 Eagleville Road
Eagleville PA 19403
Phone: (610) 278- 3441
Website:
https://www.montgomerycountypa.gov/418/Archival-Record-Retrieval

Montgomery County Courthouse
493 Swede Street
Norristown, PA 19401
Phone: (610) 278-3000
Website: https://www.montgomerycountypa.gov

***

Montour County

Montour County Courthouse
253 Mill Street
Danville, PA 17821
Phone: (570) 271-3012
Website: https://montourcounty.gov

***

Northampton County

Northampton County Courthouse
669 Washington Street
Easton, PA 18042
Phone: (610) 829-6500
Website: https://www.northamptoncounty.org

***

Northumberland County

Northumberland County Courthouse
201 Market Street
Sunbury, PA 17801
Phone: (570) 988-4148
Website: https://www.norrycopa.net

***

Perry County

Perry County Courthouse
2 East Main Street
New Bloomfield, PA 17068
Phone: (717) 582-2131
Website: https://perryco.org

***

Philadelphia

Philadelphia City Archives
548 Spring Garden Street
Philadelphia, PA 19123
Phone: (215) 685 - 9409
Website:
https://www.phila.gov/departments/department-of-records/city-archives

Philadelphia City Hall
Broad & Market Streets
Philadelphia, PA 19107
Phone: (215) 686 - 4252
Website: https://www.phila.gov

***

Pike County

Pike County Courthouse
506 Broad Street
Milford, PA 18337
Phone: (570) 296-7231
Website: https://www.pikepa.org

***

Potter County

Potter County Courthouse
1 Main Street
Coudersport, PA 16915
Phone: (814) 274-8290
Website: https://pottercountypa.net

***

Schuylkill County

Schuylkill County Courthouse Archives
401 North 2nd Street
Pottsville, PA 17801
Phone: (570) 628-1145
Website: https://schuylkillcountypa.gov

***

Snyder County

Snyder County Courthouse
9 West Market Street
Middleburg, PA 17842
Phone: (570) 837-4224
Website: https://www.snydercounty.org

***

Somerset County

Somerset County Courthouse
111 East Union Street
Somerset, PA 15501
Phone: (814) 445-1548
Website: http://www.co.somerset.pa.us

***

Sullivan County

Sullivan County Courthouse
245 Muncy Street
Laporte, PA 18626
Phone: (570) 946-7351
Website: https://www.sullivancountypa.gov

***

Susquehana County

Susquehanna County Courthouse
31 Lake Avenue
Montrose, PA 18801
Phone: (570) 278-4600
Website: https://www.susqco.com

***

Tioga County

Tioga County Courthouse
116 Main Street
Wellsboro, PA 16901
Phone: (717) 248-6733
Website: https://www.tiogacountypa.us

***

Union County

Union County Courthouse
103 South Second Street
Lewisburg, PA 17837
Phone: (570) 524-8762
Website: https://www.unioncountypa.org

***

Venango County

Venango County Courthouse
1168 Liberty Street
Franklin, PA 16323
Phone: (814) 432-9539
Website: https://www.co.venango.pa.us

***

Warren County

County of Warren
204 Fourth Avenue
Warren, PA 16365
Phone: (814) 728-3400
Website: https://warrencopa.com

***

Washington County

Washington County Courthouse
1 South Main Street
Washington, PA 15301
Phone: (724) 228-6806
Website: https://www.co.washington.pa.us

***

Wayne County

Wayne County Courthouse
925 Court Street
Honesdale, PA 18431
Phone: (570) 253-5970
Website: https://www.waynecountypa.gov

***

Westmoreland County

Westmoreland County Courthouse
2 North Main Street
Greensburg, PA 15601
Phone: (717) 248-6733
Website: https://www.co.westmoreland.pa.us

***

Wyoming County

Wyoming County Courthouse
1 Courthouse Square
Tunkhannock, PA 18657
Phone: (570) 836-3200
Website: https://wyomingcountypa.gov

***

York County

York County Archives
150 Pleasant Acres Road
York, PA 17402
Phone: (717) 840-7222
Website: https://www.yorkcountyarchives.org

York County Government
45 North George Street
York, PA 17401
Phone: (717) 771 - 9288
Website: https://yorkcountypa.gov

Chapter 8

Archives and Special Collections at Colleges and Universities

PENNSYLVANIA IS HOME TO hundreds of colleges and universities. Many of these educational institutions have special collections in their libraries, housing materials of interest to genealogists. In this chapter is a comprehensive listing of every sizable archival collection. Penn State University (University Park) and Temple University (Philadelphia) were discussed in Chapter 6: Regional Pennsylvania Archives.

Each institution has an archive dedicated to its own school's history. This can include yearbooks, campus newspapers, professors' papers, dissertations, theses, and memorabilia from student activities. This is valuable for researchers with ancestors who attended or worked at the school. Those of us without collegiate ancestors can also find images and items of the surrounding community preserved in these collections.

Remember to use Chapter 3: Using Catalogs and Finding Aids to develop your research plan. Almost all college and university archives are open to the public for research, usually without a fee. In the listings below, useful genealogy items are noted with "Features".

***

ADAMS COUNTY

Gettysburg College, Special Collections & College Archives
Website: https://www.gettysburg.edu/special-collections

***

ALLEGHENY COUNTY

Carnegie Mellon University, University Archives
Website:
https://library.cmu.edu/distinctive-collections/university-archives
Website digital collections: https://digitalcollections.library.cmu.edu

Chatham University, Jennie King Mellon Library Archives and Special Collections
Website: https://library.chatham.edu/archives

Duquesne University, University Archives and Special Collections
Website: https://guides.library.duq.edu/archives
Features: Catholic Historical Society of Western Pennsylvania collection

La Roche University, Wright Library
Website: https://library.laroche.edu

Penn State Greater Allegheny, J. Clarence Kelly Library
Website: https://libraries.psu.edu/greaterallegheny

***

BEAVER COUNTY

Geneva College, McCartney Library
Website: https://www.geneva.edu/library

Penn State Beaver, Beaver Campus Library
Website: https://libraries.psu.edu/beaver

***

BERKS COUNTY

Albright College, Archives and Special Collections
Website: https://library.albright.edu/casc

Alvernia University, Franco Library
Website: https://www.alvernia.edu/franco-library-alvernia-university

Kutztown University of Pennsylvania, Rohrbach Library
Website: https://library.kutztown.edu/home

Penn State Berks, Berks Thun Library
Website: https://libraries.psu.edu/berks

***

BLAIR COUNTY

Penn State Altoona, Robert E. Eiche Library
Website: https://libraries.psu.edu/altoona

***

Bucks County

Cairn University, Rare Books and Archives
Website: https://lib.cairn.edu

***

Butler County

Slippery Rock University, Bailey Library University Archives and Special Collections
Website: https://www.sru.edu/academics/bailey-library

***

Cambria County

Saint Francis University, University Archives
Website: https://libguides.francis.edu/archives-collections

***

Centre County

Penn State University, Main Campus
See detailed profile in Chapter 6: Regional Pennsylvania Archives

***

CHESTER COUNTY

Immaculata University, Gabriele Library
Website: https://library.immaculata.edu

Lincoln University, Langston Hughes Memorial Library
Website: https://www.lincoln.edu/langston-hughes-memorial-library/special-collections-and-archives/index.html

West Chester University, Libraries Special Collections
Website: https://library.wcupa.edu/specialcollections

***

CLARION COUNTY

Pennsylvania Western University, Archives and Collections
(Formerly Clarion University)
Website: https://library.pennwest.edu/archives

***

CLEARFIELD COUNTY

Penn State Dubois, DuBois Campus Library
Website: https://libraries.psu.edu/dubois

***

Clinton County

Lock Haven University, Commonwealth University of PA: University Archives and Special Collections
In partnership with Bloomsburg University and Mansfield University
Website: https://library.commonwealthu.edu/archives

***

Columbia County

Bloomsburg University, Commonwealth University of PA: University Archives and Special Collections
In partnership with Mansfield University and Lock Haven University
Website: https://library.commonwealthu.edu/archives

***

Crawford County

Allegheny College, Merrick Archive and Special Collections
Website: https://sites.allegheny.edu/library/special-collections

***

Cumberland County

Dickinson College, Archives & Special Collections
Website: https://archives.dickinson.edu/

Features: Civil War Resources
https://archives.dickinson.edu/civil-war

Shippensburg University, Luhrs Library
Website: https://library.ship.edu/luhrs

U.S. Army War College Heritage and Education Center
Website: https://ahec.armywarcollege.edu

***

Dauphin County

Penn State Harrisburg, Madlyn L. Hanes Library
Website: https://libraries.psu.edu/harrisburg

***

Delaware County

Cabrini University
*Closed in 2024. Villanova University holds the archives of the university.

Cheyney University of Pennsylvania, Archives
Website: https://cheyney.edu/academics/library/archive-documents

Eastern University, Warner Library Archives and Special Collections
Website: https://library.eastern.edu/archivesspecialcoll

Neumann University, Library Archives
Website: https://www.neumann.edu/academics/library/archives

Haverford College, TriCollege Libraries Archives & Manuscripts
In partnership with Bryn Mawr College and Swarthmore College

Website:
https://archives.tricolib.brynmawr.edu/repositories/5/search

Penn State Brandywine, Vairo Library
Website: https://libraries.psu.edu/brandywine

Swarthmore College, TriCollege Libraries Archives & Manuscripts
In partnership with Haverford College and Bryn Mawr College
Website:
https://archives.tricolib.brynmawr.edu/repositories/5/search
Features: Friends Historical Library with Quaker History and Genealogy https://www.swarthmore.edu/friends-historical-library

Villanova University, University Archives
Website: https://library.villanova.edu/collections/distinctive/archives
Digital exhibits: https://exhibits.library.villanova.edu

Widener University, Wolfgram Memorial Library
Website:
https://www.widener.edu/about/campus-community-resources/wolfgram-memorial-library

***

Erie County

Gannon University, Nash Library Archives
Website: https://library.gannon.edu/archives

Mercyhurst University, Archival Center
Website: https://library.mercyhurst.edu/home

Penn State Behrend, John M. Lilley Library
Website: https://libraries.psu.edu/behrend

***

Fayette County

Penn State Fayette, Campus Library
Website: https://libraries.psu.edu/fayette

***

Franklin County

Penn State Mont Alto, Campus Library
Website: https://libraries.psu.edu/montalto

Wilson College, Library
Website: https://library.wilson.edu

***

Greene County

Waynesburg University, Eberly Library
Website: https://waynesburg.libguides.com/eberly

***

Huntingdon County

Juniata College, Archives and Special Collections
Website: https://libguides.juniata.edu/ASC

***

Indiana County

Indiana University of Pennsylvania, Special Collections and University Archives
Website: https://www.iup.edu/library/departments/archives/index.html

***

Lackawanna County

Marywood University, Historical Archives
Website: https://www.marywood.edu/about/history/historical-archives/

Penn State Scranton, Scranton Campus Library
Website: https://libraries.psu.edu/scranton

University of Scranton, Archives & McHugh Family Special Collections
Website: https://digitalservices.scranton.edu
Features: Scranton local history collection

***

Lancaster County

Elizabethtown College, Hess Archives and Special Collections
Website: https://www.etown.edu/library/archives/index.aspx

Franklin & Marshall College, Archives and Special Collections
Website: https://library.fandm.edu/archives/home

Millersville University of Pennsylvania, McNairy Library Special Collections
Website: https://library.millersville.edu/home

***

Lawrence County

Westminster College, Library
Website: https://www.westminster.edu/academics/library

***

Lebanon County

Lebanon Valley College, Bishop Library
Website: https://www.lvc.edu/library/

***

Lehigh County

Cedar Crest College, Cressman Library
Website: https://www3.cedarcrest.edu/library/index.shtm

DeSales University, Trexler Library
Website: https://www.desales.edu/trexler-library

Muhlenberg Colleg,e Trexler Library Special Collections & Archives
Website:
https://trexler.muhlenberg.edu/library/specialcollections/archives

Penn State Lehigh Valley, Lehigh Valley Campus Library
Website: https://libraries.psu.edu/lehighvalley

***

Luzerne County

King's College, Corgan Library
Website: https://www.kings.edu/academics/library

Misericordia University, Bevevino Library
Website: https://www.misericordia.edu/library

Penn State Hazleton, Mary M. and Bertil E. Lofstrom Library
Website: https://libraries.psu.edu/hazleton

Penn State Wilkes-Barre, Nesbitt Library
Website: https://libraries.psu.edu/wilkesbarre

Wilkes University, Archives and Special Collections
Website: https://wilkes.libguides.com/library/archives

***

Lycoming County

Lycoming College, Snowden Library
Website: https://www.lycoming.edu/library

Mercer County

Grove City College, Buhl Library
Website: https://hbl.gcc.edu

Penn State Shenango, Lartz Memorial Library
Website: https://libraries.psu.edu/shenango

Thiel College, Archives
Website: https://www.thiel.edu/library/the-thiel-archives

***

Monroe County

East Stroudsburg University, Kemp Library Archives
Website:
https://www.esu.edu/library/collections/archives/index.cfm

***

Montgomery County

Arcadia University, Landman Library
Website: https://www.arcadia.edu/academics/landman-library-1

Bryn Athyn College, Swedenborg Library
Website: https://acns.ent.sirsi.net/client/en_US/main-csoa

Bryn Mawr College, TriCollege Libraries Archives & Manuscripts
In partnership with Haverford College and Swarthmore College
Website: https://archives.tricolib.brynmawr.edu/repositories/5/search

Gwynedd Mercy University, Keiss Library University Archives
Website: https://gmercyu.libguides.com/archives

Penn State Abington, Campus Library
Website: https://libraries.psu.edu/abington

Rosemont College, Kistler Memorial Library Archives and Special Collections
Website: https://researchguides.rosemont.edu/archives

Saint Joseph's University, Library Collections
Website: https://www.sju.edu/library/collections

Ursinus College, Archives and Special Collections
Website: https://www.ursinus.edu/offices/library-and-information-technology/library/archives-and-special-collections
Features: Pennsylvania Folklife Society Collection on early Pennsylvania Germans
https://www.ursinus.edu/offices/library-and-information-technology/library/archives-and-special-collections/pennsylvania-folklife-society-collection

***

Northampton County

Lafayette College, Special Collections & College Archives
Website: https://archives.lafayette.edu/

Lehigh University, University Archives
Website: https://libraryguides.lehigh.edu/archives/university-archives
Website digital collections:
https://digitalcollections.lib.lehigh.edu/islandora/object/digitalcollecti

ons%3Aroot
Features: Lehigh Coal and Navigation Company Records and "I Remain: A Digital Archive of Letters, Manuscripts, and Ephemera"

Moravian College, Reeves Library
Website: https://www.moravian.edu/reeves

***

PHILADELPHIA

University of Pennsylvania, University Archives & Records Center
Website: https://archives.upenn.edu/
Features: West Philadelphia community history and historical maps

University of Pennsylvania, Kislak Center for Special Collections, Rare Books and Manuscripts
Website: https://www.library.upenn.edu/kislak
Other archives at Penn:
https://archives.upenn.edu/archives-info/other-archives

Chestnut Hill College
Logue Library https://library1.chc.edu

Drexel University, Archives
Website: https://www.library.drexel.edu/archives/overview

Drexel University: Legacy Center Archives & Special Collections College of Medicine
Website: https://drexel.edu/legacy-center
Features: Records of Woman's Medical College, Hahnemann University

La Salle University, Connelly Library
Website: https://library.lasalle.edu

Thomas Jefferson University, University Archives
(Philadelphia University merged with Thomas Jefferson University)

Website:
https://library.jefferson.edu/archives/collections/archives.cfm

***

Schuylkill County

Penn State Schuylkill, Ciletti Memorial Library
Website: https://libraries.psu.edu/schuylkill

***

Snyder County

Susquehana University, Blough-Weis Library
Website: https://library.susqu.edu/home

***

Tioga County

Mansfield University, Commonwealth University of PA: University Archives and Special Collections
In partnership with Bloomsburg University and Lock Haven University
Website: https://library.commonwealthu.edu/archives

***

Union County

Bucknell University, Special Collections/University Archives
Website: https://researchbysubject.bucknell.edu/scua

***

Venango County

Pennsylvania Western University, Archives and Collections
(Formerly Clarion University)
Website: https://library.pennwest.edu/archives

***

Washington County

Pennsylvania Western University, Archives and Collections
(Formerly Edinboro University, California University)
Website: https://library.pennwest.edu/archives

Washington & Jefferson University, Clark Family Library
Website: https://libguides.washjeff.edu/home

***

Westmoreland County

Penn State New Kensington, Elisabeth S. Blissell Library
Website: https://libraries.psu.edu/newkensington

***

York County

Penn State York, Lee R. Glatfelter Library
Website: https://libraries.psu.edu/york

Seton Hill University, Reeves Memorial Library
Website: https://setonhill.libguides.com/library

York College of Pennsylvania, Schmidt Library Archives and Special Collections
Website: https://library.ycp.edu/home

Chapter 9

Local Organizational, Historical, and Genealogical Archives

LOCAL ARCHIVES IN PENNSYLVANIA are those which focus on collecting materials for their county, city, township, borough, community, historical site or figure, genealogical society, industry, activity, or ethnic group. These are often volunteer-run non-profit organizations, and do not typically employ professional archivists for processing their materials. However, their collections are highly focused and specific, offering rich details about the past that are not found elsewhere. If you have an ancestor connected to one of these places, people, or activities, there is a good chance there is a record of him or her there.

The local archives listed below are organized geographically by county. What is not listed in this section is the county courthouses and county government archives holding historical courthouse records, such as wills, deeds, court records, etc. For that list, consult Chapter 7: County Courthouses and Archives.

To save space, physical addresses are not provided, but website addresses are. Researchers are encouraged to visit each website for more details on archival holdings and how to research its collections.

***

Adams County

Adams County Historical Society and Beyond the Battle Museum
Website: https://www.achs-pa.org

American Museum of Military History
Website: https://www.museumofmilitaryhistory.com

Biglerville Historical and Preservation Society
Website: https://www.facebook.com/Biglerville-Historical-and-Preservation-Society-1958759457734710

East Berlin Historical Preservation Society
Website: http://ebhpspa.org

General Lee's Headquarters Museum
Website: https://www.battlefields.org/visit/heritage-sites/gettysburg-battlefield-general-lees-headquarters

Gettysburg Battlefield Preservation Association
Website: https://www.gbpa.org

Gettysburg Foundation Museum and Visitor Center
Website: https://www.gettysburgfoundation.org/museum-visitor-center

Gettysburg National Military Park
Website: https://www.nps.gov/gett/learn/historyculture/collections.htm

John T. Reily Historical Society
Website: https://www.jtrhs.org

Seminary Ridge Museum
Website: https://www.seminaryridgeeducation.org

Shriver House Museum
Website: http://shriverhouse.org

Ye Old Sulphur Spa Historical Society
Website: https://www.yosshs.org

***

Allegheny County

Afro-American Historical and Genealogical Society
Website: https://www.aahgs.org

Allegheny Cemetery Historical Association
Website: https://alleghenycemetery.com

Allegheny Foothills Historical Society
Website: http://plumhistory.org

Allegheny-Kiski Valley Historical Society
Website: http://akvhs.org

August Wilson Center for African American Culture
Website: http://www.augustwilsoncenter.org

Bayernhof Museum
Website: http://www.bayernhofmuseum.com

Bloomfield Preservation and Heritage Society
Website: http://www.bloomfieldlive.com/bloomfield-preservation--heritage-society.html

Carrick-Overbrook Historical Society
Website: http://www.carrick-overbrook.org

Coraopolis Historical Society
Website: https://www.facebook.com/coraopolishistory

The Daguerreian Society
Website: https://lebohistory.org

Depreciation Lands Museum
Website: http://dlmuseum.org

Edgewood Historical Society
Website: https://www.facebook.com/EdgewoodHistoricalSociety

Elizabeth Township Historical Society
Website: https://www.facebook.com/ElizabethTownshipHistoricalSociety

Fort Pitt Museum
Website: https://www.heinzhistorycenter.org/fort-pitt

Frick Art and Historical Center
Website: http://www.thefrickpittsburgh.org

Heinz History Center
Website: http://www.heinzhistorycenter.org

Historical Society of Carnegie
Website: https://www.facebook.com/HistoricalSocietyofCarnegie

Historical Society of Green Tree
Website: http://www.greentreeboro.com/histsoc.php

Jewish Genealogical Society of Pittsburgh
Website: https://www.pghjgs.org

Historical Society of Mt. Lebanon
Website: https://lebohistory.org

Historical Society of Upper St. Clair
Website: https://www.hsusc.org

Lawrenceville Historical Society
Website: https://www.lawrencevillehistoricalsociety.org

Manchester Historic Society
Website: http://www.manchesterhistoricsocietypa.com

Mexican War Streets Society
Website: http://www.mexicanwarstreets.org

McKees Rocks Historical Society
Website: https://www.facebook.com/McKees-Rocks-Historical-Society-139655842733617

McKeesport Preservation Society
Website: https://www.facebook.com/McKeesportPS

McKeesport Regional History and Heritage Center
Website: https://www.mckeesportheritage.org

North Hills Genealogists
Website: http://www.northhillsgenealogists.org

Old Moon Township Historical Society
Website: https://moontownshiphistoricalsociety.com

Rachel Carson Homestead Association
Website: http://www.rachelcarsonhomestead.org

Rivers of Steel Heritage Corporation (Carrie Furnace)
Website: http://www.riversofsteel.com

Saint David's Welsh Society of Pittsburgh
Website: https://www.stdavidssociety.org

Sewickley Heights History Center
Website: https://www.sewickleyheightshistory.org

Sewickley Valley Historical Society
Website: http://sewickleyhistory.org

Soldiers and Sailors Memorial Hall and Museum
Website: https://www.soldiersandsailorshall.org

South Park Historical Society
Website: http://www.southparkhistoricalsociety.com

Squirrel Hill Historical Society
Website: http://www.squirrelhillhistory.org

Tarentum History and Landmarks Foundation
Website:

https://www.facebook.com/Tarentum-History-With-Cindy-387764171353675

Theatre Historical Society of America
Website: https://historictheatres.org

Tour-Ed Mine and Museum
Website: https://tour-edmine.com

Turtle Creek Valley Historical Society
Website: https://www.facebook.com/TCHistorical

Verona Historical Society
Website: http://www.veronahistory.org

Western Pennsylvania Genealogical Society
Website: http://www.wpgs.org

***

Armstrong County

Apollo Area Historical Society
Website: https://apollopahistory.com

Armstrong County Historical Museum and Genealogical Society
Website: https://www.achmgs.org

Brady's Bend Historical Society
Website: http://www.bradysbendhistoricalsociety.org

Dayton Area Local History Society
Website: http://daytonpa.org

Freeport Area Historical Society
Website: https://www.freeporthistoricalsociety.org

Leechburg Area Museum and Historical Society
Website: https://leechburgmuseum.org

Beaver County

Beaver Area Historical Museum
Website:
https://www.bcpahistory.org/beavercounty/HistoricalSocieties/Beaver/Beaver.html

Beaver County Genealogy and History Center
Website:
https://www.facebook.com/profile.php?id=100057099144268

Beaver Falls Historical Society and Museum
Website:
https://www.facebook.com/Beaver-Falls-Historical-Museum-745367992315864

Brighton Township Historical Society
Website: https://brightontwp.org/historical-society

Harmonie Associates
Website: https://www.harmonie.org

Little Beaver Historical Society
Website: https://littlebeaverhistorical.org

National Iron and Steel Heritage Museum
Website: https://steelmuseum.org

New Brighton Historical Society
Website: https://www.nbhistory.org

Old Economy Village
Website: http://oldeconomyvillage.org

Research and Resource Center for Beaver County
Website: https://bchrlf.org

Richmond Little Red Schoolhouse Association
Website: https://brightontwp.org/little-red-school-house

South Side Historical Village
Website: https://www.facebook.com/South.Side.Historic.Village

***

Bedford County

Anderson House
Website: https://www.societyofthecincinnati.org/larz-and-isabel-anderson

Bedford County Historical Society
Website: http://www.bedfordpahistory.com

Cumberland Valley Township Historical Society
Website: https://www.visitcumberlandvalley.com/listing/cumberland-county-historical-society/792

Fort Bedford Museum
Website: http://www.fortbedfordmuseum.org

Old Bedford Village
Website: http://www.oldbedfordvillage.com

***

Berks County

Albany Township Historical Society
Website: https://www.albanyths.org

ARCHIVES IN PENNSYLVANIA FOR GENEALOGY RESEARCH 139

American Museum of Veterinary Medicine
Website: https://www.avmhs.org/veterinary-museums-and-exhibits

Berks County Genealogical Society
Website: https://berksgenes.org

Berks History
Website: https://www.berkshistory.org

Boyertown Area Historical Society
Website: http://www.boyertownhistory.org

Conrad Weiser Homestead
Website: http://www.conradweiserhomestead.org

Fleetwood Area Historical Society
Website: https://fleetwoodpa.org

Hay Creek Valley Historical Association and Joanna Iron Furnace
Website: http://www.haycreek.org

Heidelberg Heritage Society
Website: https://www.heidelbergsociety.org

Kutztown Area Historical Society
Website: http://www.kutztownhistory.org

Mid Atlantic Air Museum
Website: http://www.maam.org

Oley Valley Heritage Association
Website: https://www.oleyvalleyheritage.org/site

Pennsylvania German Cultural Heritage Center
Website: https://www.kutztown.edu/about-ku/our-campus/maps/pennsylvania-german-cultural-heritage-center.html

Pine Forge Historical Society
Website: https://pine-forgehs.org/

Reading Area Firefighters Museum Inc
Website: http://www.readingpafiremuseum.com

Reading Public Museum
Website: http://www.readingpublicmuseum.org

Reading Railroad Heritage Museum
Website: http://www.readingrailroad.org

Sinking Spring Historical Society
Website: https://www.facebook.com/Sinking-Spring-Area-Historical-Society-and-Heritage-Park-101603801315574

Tulpehocken Settlement Historical Society
Website: https://tulpehockenroots.org

***

Blair County

Altoona Railroaders Memorial Museum
Website: https://www.railroadcity.org

Baker Mansion Museum
Website: http://www.blairhistory.org

Blair County Genealogical Society
Website: http://www.bcgslibrary.org

Blair County Historical Society
Website: http://www.blairhistory.org

Fort Roberdeau Association
Website: https://fortroberdeau.org

Bellwood -Antis Historical Society
Website: http://www.bellwoodantis.net/history.html

Railroader's Heritage Corporation
Website: https://www.railroadcity.org

Roaring Spring Historical Society
Website: https://www.facebook.com/RSHistoricalSociety

Tyrone Area Historical Society
Website: http://www.tyronehistory.org

Williamsburg Heritage and Historical Society
Website: https://sites.google.com/site/williamsburgpennsylvania/history-historical-district-information

***

Bradford County

Bradford County Heritage Association
Website: https://theheritagevillage.org

Bradford County Historical Society
Website: http://bradfordhistory.com

Sayre Historical Society
Website: https://sayrehistoricalsociety.org

Tioga Point Museum
Website: http://www.TiogaPointMuseum.com

Tuscarora Township Historical Society
Website: https://sites.psu.edu/ourstorycentralpausnewspaperproject/vignettes/tuscarora-township-historical-society

Wyalusing Valley Museum Association, Inc.
Website: https://www.facebook.com/wyalusingmuseum

***

Bucks County

Andalusia Foundation
Website: http://andalusiapa.org

Bristol Cultural and Historical Foundation
Website: https://www.bristolhistory.org

Bucks County Civil War Round Table Museum and Library
Website: http://www.civilwarmuseumdoylestown.org

Bucks County Genealogical Society
Website: https://bucksgen.org

Bucks County Historical Society
Website: https://www.mercermuseum.org/about/press-room/fact-sheet-bchs-2

Craven Hall Historical Society, Inc.
Website: https://craven-hall.org

Doylestown Historical Society
Website: https://doylestownhistorical.org

Dublin Historical Society
Website: https://dublinohiohistory.org

Haycock Historical Society
Website: https://haycockhistoricalsociety.org

Historical Society of Bensalem Township
Website: http://bensalemhistoricalsociety.com

Historical Society of Hilltown Township
Website: https://www.hilltownhistory.org

Historic Morrisville Society
Website: https://historicsummerseat.com

Hulmeville Historical Society, Inc.
Website: http://www.hulmevillehistorical.org

John Fitch Steamboat Museum
Website: https://craven-hall.org/fitch-steamboat-museum

Johnsville Centrifuge and Science Museum
Website: https://nadcmuseum.org

Levittown Historical Society
Website: https://www.facebook.com/Levittown-Historical-Society-And-Museum-1364661420227399

Lower Makefield Township Historical Society
Website: https://www.lmt.org/government/boards-and-commissions/historical-commission

Margaret R. Grundy Memorial Museum
Website: http://www.grundymuseum.org

New Hope Historical Society
Website: https://newhopehistorical.org

Newtown Historic Association
Website: http://www.newtownhistoric.org

Northampton Township Historical Society
Website: https://www.northamptontownshiphistoricalsociety.org

Patterson Farm Preservation
Website: http://www.pattersonfarmpreservation.com

Pearl S. Buck International House and Historic Site
Website: http://www.pearlsbuck.org

Pennsbury Manor
Website: https://www.pennsburymanor.org

Pennsylvania Postal History Society
Website: http://www.paphs.org

Perkasie Historical Society
Website: https://www.perkasiehistory.org

Plumstead Historical Society
Website: https://sites.google.com/site/plumsteadhistoricalsocietyorg

Quakertown HIstorical Society
Website: https://www.quakertownhistoricalsociety.org

Richland Historical Society
Website: https://richlandcountyhistoricalsociety.weebly.com

Sellersville Museum
Website: http://www.sellersvillemuseum.org

Solebury Township Historical Society
Website: http://soleburyhistory.org

Springfield Township Historical Society
Website: http://www.springfieldbucks.org/township_facts.php

Warwick Township Historical Society
Website: http://www.moland.org

Washington Crossing Historic Park
Website: https://www.washingtoncrossingpark.org

Yardley Historical Association
Website: http://www.yardleyhistory.org

***

Butler County

Butler County Genealogical Society
Website: https://butlercountyogs.org

Butler County Historical Society
Website: https://butlerhistory.com

Cranberry Township Historical Society
Website: https://explorecranberry.org

Cranberry Genealogy Society
Website: https://www.cranberrygenealogy.org

John Roebling's Historic Saxonburg Society
Website: https://www.facebook.com/JRHSS

Maridon Museum
Website: http://www.maridon.org

Mars Area History and Landmarks Society
Website: https://marshistory.org

Slippery Rock Heritage Association
Website: http://srheritage.org

Zelienople Historical Society
Website: https://www.zeliehistory.org

***

CAMBRIA COUNTY

Allegheny Portage Railroad National Historic Site
Website: https://www.nps.gov/alpo/index.htm

Cambria County Historical Society
Website: http://www.cambriacountyhistorical.com

Flood Museum
Website: https://www.thefloodmuseum.com

The Inclined Plane, Inc.
Website: http://www.inclinedplane.org

Lilly Washington Historical Society
Website: https://l-whs.org

Portage Area Historical Society
Website: https://www.facebook.com/Portageareahistoricalsociety

Tunnels Park and Museum
Website: http://www.gallitzin.info

Windber-Johnstown Area Genealogical Society
Website: http://www.johnstownroots.org

***

Cameron County

Cameron County Historical Society
Website: https://cameroncohistorical.wixsite.com/cameroncohistorysoc

***

Carbon County

Asa Packer Mansion
Website: http://www.asapackermansion.com

Lansford Historical Society
Website: http://lansfordhistoricalsociety.weebly.com/index.html

Mauch Chunk Museum
Website: https://mauchchunkmcc.org

No. 9 Washanty Mine and Museum
Website: https://no9minemuseum.wixsite.com/museum

Old Jail Museum and Heritage Center
Website: http://www.theoldjailmuseum.com

Palmerton Area Historical Society
Website: https://www.palmertonhistorical.org

Summit Hill Historical Society and Museum
Website: https://www.facebook.com/summithill

***

Centre County

Bellefonte Museum for Centre County
Website: https://www.bellefontemuseum.org

Boalsburg Heritage Museum
Website: https://www.boalsburgheritagemuseum.org

Boal Mansion Museum
http://www.boalmuseum.com

Centre County Genealogical Society
Website: https://centrecountygenealogy.org

Centre County Historical Society
Website: https://centrehistory.org

Centre County Library and Historical Museum
Website: https://www.centrecountylibrary.org

Eagle Iron Works and Curtin Village
Website: https://www.curtinvillage.com

Milesburg Historical Society
Website: https://www.milesburg.org

Penns Valley Area Historical Museum Association
Website: http://www.pennsvalleymuseum.org

Pennsylvania Military Museum
Website: http://www.pamilmuseum.org

Philipsburg Historical Foundation
Website: https://www.phf1797.com

***

Chester County

Alfred O. Deshong Museum and Cultural Arts Center
Website: http://www.oldchesterpa.com/museum_deshong.htm

Caln Township Historical Society
Website: https://www.oldcalnhistoricalsociety.org

Charlestown Historical Society
Website: https://www.charlestownhistorical.org

Chester County History Center
Website: https://mycchc.org

Downingtown Area Historical Society
Website: http://www.downingtownareahistoricalsociety.org

Historical Society of the Phoenixville Area
Website: http://www.phoenixvillehistoricalsociety.org

Kennett Square Historical Commission
Website: https://www.kennett.pa.us/199/Historical-Commission

Kennett Underground Railroad Center
Website: https://www.kennettundergroundrr.org

National Iron and Steel Heritage Museum
Website: http://www.steelmuseum.org

Old Caln Historical Society
Website: https://www.oldcalnhistoricalsociety.org

Oxford Area Historical Association
Website: http://www.oxfordhistorical.org

Schuylkill Township Historical Commission
Website: http://www.schuylkilltwp.org

Tredyffrin Easttown Historical Society
Website: http://www.tehistory.org

Tredyffrin Historic Preservation Trust
Website: https://tredyffrinhistory.org/?page_id=327

Tri-County Heritage Society
Website: https://haycreek.org/tricounty-heritage-society

Welkinweir
Website: http://www.welkinweir.org

West Whiteland Historical Commission/Friends of the Thomas Mill
Website: https://www.westwhiteland.org/180/Historical-Commission

Wharton Esherick Museum
Website: http://www.whartonesherickmuseum.org

***

Clarion County

Clarion County Historical Society
Website: http://www.clarioncountyhistoricalsociety.org

***

CLEARFIELD COUNTY

Clearfield County Historical Society
Website: http://www.clearfield-county-historical-society.net

Coalport Area Coal Museum
Website: http://www.coalportmuseum.org

DuBois Area Historical Society
Website: http://duboishs.com

East Broad Top RR Preservation Association
Website: https://eastbroadtop.com

***

CLINTON COUNTY

Clinton County Historical Society
Website: https://www.facebook.com/CCHSofPA

Greater Renovo Area Historical Society
Website: https://renovoheritage.org

Piper Aviation Museum Foundation
Website: http://www.pipermuseum.com

Sugar Valley Historical Society
Website: http://www.svhistory.org

***

COLUMBIA COUNTY

Berwick Historical Society
Website: https://berwickhistoricalsociety.org

Columbia County Historical Society
Website: http://www.colcohist-gensoc.org

Red Deer at Rolling Hills Farm
Website: http://www.reddeeratrollinghillsfarm.com

***

CRAWFORD COUNTY

Baldwin-Reynolds House Museum
Website: http://www.baldwinreynolds.org

Conneaut Lake Area Historical Society
Website: https://www.conneautlakehistory.com

Crawford County Historical Society
Website: http://www.crawfordhistorical.org/chs

Drake Well Museum
Website: http://www.drakewell.org

Johnson-Shaw Stereoscopic Museum
Website: http://www.johnsonshawmuseum.org

John Brown Farm, Tannery and Museum
Website: https://visitcrawford.org/listing/john-brown-tannery-site

Linesville Historical Society
Website: https://www.countyoffice.org/linesville-historical-society-linesville-pa-af1

Northwestern PA Railroad and Tooling Heritage Center
Website: https://www.facebook.com/NWPAHeritagePartnership

Oil Creek Railway Historical Society
Website: https://octrr.org

Titusville Historical Society
Website: https://titusvillehistoricalsociety.org

***

Cumberland County

Cumberland County Historical Society and Hamilton Library
Website: https://www.historicalsociety.com/visit/museum

Historical Society of East Pennsboro Inc
Website: http://www.ephistory.org

Newville Historical Society
Website: https://newvillehistoricalsociety.weebly.com

Shippensburg Historical Society
Website: https://www.shippensburghistoricalsociety.org

***

Dauphin County

Camp Curtin Historical Society
Website: https://www.campcurtin.org

Capital Area Genealogical Society
Website: http://capitalareagenealogy.org

Dauphin Middle-Paxton Historical Society
Website: http://capitalareagenealogy.org

Gratz Historical Society
Website: http://capitalareagenealogy.org

Halifax Area Historical Society
Website: https://www.facebook.com/Halifax-Area-Historical-Society-128563587613

Hershey Derry Township Historical Society
Website: http://www.hersheyhistory.com

Highspire Historical Society
Website: http://highspirehistory.org/index.html

Historical Society of Dauphin County
Website: http://www.dauphincountyhistory.org

Historical Society of East Hanover Township
Website: https://www.facebook.com/Historical-Society-of-East-Hanover-Township-Dauphin-County-1689373737828430

Historical Society of Millersburg and Upper Paxton Township
Website: https://www.millersburghistory.com

Hummelstown Area Historical Society
Website: https://www.hummelstownhistoricalsociety.org

Londonderry Township Historical Society
Website: https://www.londonderrypa.org/#gsc.tab=0

Milton Hershey School
Website: https://www.mhskids.org/about/history/school-history-department

National Civil War Museum
Website: http://www.nationalcivilwarmuseum.org

Pennsylvania Capitol Preservation Committee
Website: http://cpc.state.pa.us

Pennsylvania Fire Museum
Website: https://pnfm.org

Pennsylvania State Police Museum
Website: https://www.psp-hemc.org

Pillow Historical Society
Website: https://www.pillowhistoricalsociety.org

State Museum of Pennsylvania
Website: https://statemuseumpa.org

West Hanover Township Historical Society
Website: https://www.facebook.com/westhanoverhistorical

Williamstown Historical Society
Website: https://www.facebook.com/Williamstown-PA-Historical-Society-148329449083914

***

Delaware County

1696 Thomas Massey House
Website: http://thomasmasseyhouse.org

Aston Township Historical Society
Website: http://www.athsdelco.org

Bethel Township Preservation Society
Website: https://www.facebook.com/betheltownshippreservationsociety

Brandywine Battlefield Park Associates
Website: http://brandywinebattlefield.org

Brandywine River Museum
Website: http://www.brandywinemuseum.org

Chadds Ford Historical Society
Website: http://www.chaddsfordhistory.org

Christian C. Sanderson Museum
Website: http://www.sandersonmuseum.org

Concord Township Historical Society
Website: https://concordhist.org

Dabbs Woodfin Library and Archives at Newlin Grist Mill
Website: http://www.newlingristmill.org

Darby Borough Historical Preservation Society
Website: http://darbyhistory.com

Delaware County Historical Society
Website: https://www.padelcohistory.org

Friends Historical Association
Website: https://www.quakerhistory.org

Haverford Township Historical Society
Website: http://www.haverfordhistoricalsociety.org

Marple Historical Society
Website: http://www.marplehistoricalsociety.org

Middletown Township Historical Society
Website: http://mthsdelco.org

Nether Providence Historical Society
Website: http://nphistory.org

Newtown Square Historical Society
Website: https://nshistory.org

Norwood Historical Society
Website: http://norwoodpahistorical.org

Paper Mill House Museum
Website: https://www.facebook.com/papermillhouse

Pennhurst Memorial and Preservation Alliance
Website: http://www.preservepennhurst.org

Pennsylvania Veterans Museum
Website: https://paveteransmuseum.org

Radnor Historical Society
Website: https://radnorhistory.org

Ridley Park Historical Society
Website: https://ridleyparkhistorical.org

Rose Valley Historical Society
Website: https://rosevalleymuseum.org

Sharon Hill Historical Society
Website: https://www.facebook.com/profile.php?id=100071468263223

Swarthmore Historical Society
Website: https://www.swarthmore.edu/friends-historical-library/swarthmore-historical-society-archives

Thornbury Historical Society
Website: https://sites.google.com/site/thornburyhistoricalsociety

Tinicum Township Historical Society
Website: https://www.tinicumtwpdelco.com/historical-society

Upper Chichester Historical Society
Website: https://chichesterhistory.org

Upper Darby Historical Society
Website: http://udhistory.org

Washington-Rochambeau Revolutionary Route
Website: http://www.w3r-us.org

***

Elk County

Bucksgahuda And Western Railroad Museum
Website: http://www.bnwrr.com

Elk County Historical Society
Website: https://elkcountyhistoricalsociety.org

Historical Society of St. Mary's and Benzinger Twp
Website: http://smhistoricalsociety.com

Jones Township Historical Society
Website: https://elkcountyhistoricalsociety.org

Ridgeway Heritage Council
Website: https://www.facebook.com/people/Ridgway-Heritage-Council/100064411135160

Mt. Zion Historical Society
Website: http://mtzionhistoricalsociety.org/index.htm

***

Erie County

Corry Area Historical Society
Website: https://www.corryareahistoricalsociety.org

Edinboro Area Historical Society
Website: https://www.facebook.com/eahs.pa

Erie County Historical Society
Website: https://www.eriehistory.org

Erie Maritime Museum
Website: https://www.eriemaritimemuseum.org

Erie Society for Genealogical Research
Website: https://www.genealogyerie.org

Fairview Area Historical Society
Website: https://fairviewhistory.org

Fort Le Boeuf Historical Society
Website: https://fortleboeufhistory.com

Hagen History Center
Website: https://www.eriehistory.org

Harborcreek Historical Society
Website: https://www.harborcreekhistory.org

Harry T. Burleigh Society
Website: https://www.facebook.com/burleighsoc

Hazel Kibler Museum
Website: https://www.facebook.com/Hazel-Kibler-Museum-134111706605966

Lake Shore Railway Historical Society
Website: https://lakeshorerailway.com

Lawrence Park Historical Society
Website: https://www.facebook.com/Lawrence-Park-Historical-Society-643116839221101

North East Historical Society
Website: http://www.northeasthistoricalsociety.org

Union City Area Historical Museum
Website: https://unioncitypa.us/museum

Waitsburg Historical Society, Inc.
Website: https://www.waitsburgmuseum.org

***

Fayette County

Braddock Road Preservation Association
Website: https://braddockroadpa.org

Brownsville Historical Society and Nemacolin Castle
Website: https://www.nemacolincastle.net

Bullskin Township Historical Society
Website: https://www.bullskintownshiphistoricalsociety.org

Coal and Coke Heritage Center
Website: https://fayette.psu.edu/visit/coalandcoke

Connellsville Area Historical Society
Website: https://connellsvillehistoricalsociety.com/home

Dunbar Historical Society
Website: http://www.dunbarhistoricalsociety.com

Fayette County Genealogical Society
Website: https://www.facebook.com/FayetteGenSociety

Fayette County Historical Society
Website: https://fayettehistoricalsociety.com

Flatiron Building Heritage Center
Website: http://barcpa.org

Friendship Hill Association
Website: https://www.friendshiphillnhs.org

Fort Mason Historical Society
Website: http://www.masontownpa.com/Organizations/HistoricalSociety.aspx

Greater Tri Town Area Historical Society
Website: https://www.facebook.com/The-Greater-Tri-Town-Area-Historical-Society-284383628386118

Smock Historical Society
Website: https://www.franklinfayette.com/community/smock-historical-society

***

Forest County

Forest County Historical Society
Website: https://forestcountypahistory.org

***

Franklin County

Allison-Antrim Museum, Inc
Website: https://greencastlemuseum.org

Fort Loudon Historical Society
Website: https://www.facebook.com/fortloudounpa

Franklin County Historical Society
Website: https://www.franklinhistorical.org

Mercersburg Historical Society
Website: https://mercersburghistory.org

Old Jail and Museum
Website: https://www.franklinhistorical.org/old-jail

Pennsylvania Forest Heritage Association
Website: http://www.paforestfiremuseum.com

Renfrew Museum and Park
Website: http://www.renfrewmuseum.org

Waynesboro Historical Society
Website: http://www.waynesborohistory.com

***

FULTON COUNTY

Fulton County Historical Society Museum
Website: http://www.fultonhistory.org

***

GREENE COUNTY

Cornerstone Genealogical Society
Website: https://cornerstonegenealogy.com

Greene County Historical Society
Website: https://www.gchistory.org

Nathanael Green Historical Foundation
Website: http://www.natgreene.org/about-us.html

Paul R. Stewart Museum
Website: http://www.waynesburg.edu/museum

***

HUNTINGDON COUNTY

Broad Top Area Coal Miners Historical Society
Website: https://broadtopminersmuseum.com

Fort Shirley Heritage Association
Website: https://huntingdonhistory.org/links/fort-shirley-heritabe-association

Huntingdon County Historical Society
Website: http://www.huntingdonhistory.org

Isett Acres Museum
Website: https://isettacres.com

Mount Union Area Historical Society
Website: https://huntingdonhistory.org/links/mount-union-area-historical-society

Orbisonia/Rockhill Furnace Historical Society
Website: https://www.facebook.com/ORFHS

Rockhill Trolley Museum
Website: http://www.rockhilltrolley.org

Three Springs Area Historical Society
Website: https://www.facebook.com/ThreeSpringsSaltilloHistoricalSociety

***

Indiana County

Dane Castle Museum
Website: https://castlesy.com/dane-castle-strongstown-pennsylvania

Historical and Genealogical Society of Indiana County
Website: http://www.hgsic.org

Historical Society of the Blairsville Area
Website: https://blairsvillehistoric.com

Jimmy Stewart Museum
Website: https://jimmy.org

John G. Schmick Museum
Website: https://www.visitindianacountypa.org/members/john-g-schmick-heritage-center

Pennsylvania Labor History Society
Website: https://palaborhistorysociety.org

Saltsburg Stone House Museum
Website: http://www.saltsburgstonehousemuseum.org

Smicksburg Area Heritage Society
Website: https://www.facebook.com/Smicksburg-Area-Heritage-Society-1815265842083812

***

JEFFERSON COUNTY

Brockway Area Historical Society
Website: https://brockwayhistory.org

Coolspring Power Museum
Website: http://coolspringpowermuseum.org

Jefferson County Historical Center
Website: http://www.jchconline.org/Default.aspx

Punxsutawney Area Historical and Genealogical Society
Website: http://www.punxsyhistory.org

Reynoldsville Historical Society
Website: https://reynoldsvillehistoricalsociety.org

Juniata County

Juniata County Historical Society
Website: http://www.juniatacountyhistoricalsociety.org

Juniata Mennonite Historical Center
Website: http://www.juniatamennonitehistoricalcenter.com

Tuscarora Academy Museum
Website: https://juniatacountyhistoricalsociety.org/tuscarora-academy-museum

***

Lackawanna County

Anthracite Historic Discovery Center
Website: https://www.facebook.com/AnthraciteHistoricalDiscoveryCenter

Carbondale Historical Society and Museum, Inc.
Website: https://carbondalepahistorical.org

Electric City Trolley Museum and Station
Website: http://www.ectma.org

Greenfield Township Historical Society
Website: https://www.facebook.com/GreenfieldTownshipHistoricalSociety

Lackawanna and Wyoming Valley Railway Historical Society
Website: http://lwvrhs.org/

Lackawanna County Historical Society
Website: http://lackawannahistory.org/index.html

Pennsylvania Anthracite Heritage Museum
Website: http://www.anthracitemuseum.org

Steamtown National Historic Site
Website: https://www.nps.gov/stea/index.htm

Tripp House
Website: http://tripphouse.com

***

Lancaster County

Amos Herr House Foundation and Historical Society
Website: http://herrhomestead.org

Caernarvon Historical Society
Website: https://www.facebook.com/people/Caernarvon-Historical-Society/100027226827139

Columbia Historic Preservation Society
Website: https://www.facebook.com/Columbia-Historic-Preservation-Society-236107089521

Conestoga Area Historical Society
Website: http://www.pennmanorhistory.org

Demuth Museums and Lancaster Museum of Art
Website: https://www.demuth.org

East Petersburg Historical Society
Website: https://www.facebook.com/EastPeteHistory

Elizabethtown Historical Society
Website: https://www.facebook.com/ElizabethtownHistoricalSociety

Ephrata Cloister
Website: https://ephratacloister.org

First National Bank Museum
Website: http://www.bankmuseum.org

Historical Society of the Cocalico Valley
Website: https://www.cocalicovalleyhs.org

Historical Society of Salisbury Township
Website: http://www.salisburytwphistory.org

Lancaster County Museums Council
Website: https://lancastercountymuseums.org

Lancaster Mennonite Historical Society (now Mennonite Life)
Website: http://lmhs.org

LancasterHistory.org and Wheatland
Website: http://www.lancasterhistory.org

Landis Valley Village and Farm Museum
Website: http://www.landisvalleymuseum.org

Lititz Historical Foundation
Website: http://www.lititzhistoricalfoundation.com

Lititz Moravian Archives Museum
Website: https://www.lititzmoravian.org/museumarchivestours

The Manheim Historical Society
Website: https://manheimhistoricalsociety.org

Marietta Museum
Website: http://www.mariettarestoration.org

Maytown Historical Society
Website: https://maytownhistory.com

Millersville Area Historical Society
Website: https://www.facebook.com/minersvilleareahistoricalsociety

Mount Joy Area Historical Society
Website: https://www.facebook.com/minersvilleareahistoricalsociety

North Museum of Natural History and Science
Website: http://www.northmuseum.org

Railroad Museum of Pennsylvania
Website: https://rrmuseumpa.org/

Rock Ford Plantation And Museum
Website: http://www.rockfordplantation.org

Rough and Tumble Engineer's Historical Museum
Website: https://roughandtumble.org/

Southern Lancaster County Historical Society
Website: http://www.southernlancasterhistory.org/robert-fulton-birthplace

Strasburg Heritage Society
Website: https://strasburgheritagesociety.org

Theodore Burr Covered Bridge Society of PA
Website: http://tbcbspa.com

William Montgomery House
Website: https://themontgomeryhouse.com

Winters Heritage House Museum and The Seibert Genealogy Research Library
Website: http://www.elizabethtownhistory.org

Wright's Ferry Mansion
Website: https://lancastercountymuseums.org/wrights-ferry-mansion

***

Lawrence County

Ellwood City Historical Society
Website: https://ellwoodhistory.org

Enon Valley Community Historical Society
Website: https://www.facebook.com/enonhistoricalsociety

Lawrence County Historical Society
Website: http://www.lawrencechs.com

S.N.P.J. Slovenian Heritage Center
Website: http://snpjheritage.org

Wampum Area Historical Society, Inc.
Website: https://www.facebook.com/Wampum-Area-Historical-Society-105034050905786

***

Lebanon County

Cornwall Iron Furnace
Website: http://www.cornwallironfurnace.org

Isaac Meier Homestead
Website: https://www.facebook.com/meierhomestead/

Lebanon County Historical Society
Website: https://lebanoncountyhistory.org/

Mount Gretna Area Historical Society
Website: https://mtgretnahistory.org/

Stoy Museum
Website: https://lebanoncountyhistory.org/

***

Lehigh County

1803 House
Website: https://www.1803house.org

Coopersburg Historical Society
Website: https://www.facebook.com/coopersburghistoricalsociety

Emmaus Historical Society
Website: https://www.emmaushistoricalsociety.org

Governor Wolf Historical Society
Website: https://www.govwolf.org

Haines Mill Museum
Website: https://delawareandlehigh.org/map/attraction/haines-mill-museum

Lehigh County Historical Society
Website: http://www.lehighvalleyheritagemuseum.org

Liberty Bell Museum
Website: https://www.facebook.com/LibertyBellMuseum

Lower Macungie Township Historical Society
Website: https://www.lmthistory.org

Lower Milford Historical Society
Website: https://www.facebook.com/LMHS.PA

Lynn-Heidelberg Township Historical Society
Website: https://www.facebook.com/LHTHS

Lynn Township Historical Society
Website: https://www.lynntwp.org/about/history

Macungie Historical Society Inc.
Website: http://www.macungie.org

Museum of Indian Culture
Website: https://www.museumofindianculture.org

Shelter House Society
Website: https://shelterhouseemmaus.org

Whitehall Historic Preservation Society
Website: https://www.whitehallhistoricalsociety.org

***

Luzerne County

Eckley Miners' Village
Website: http://eckleyminersvillage.com

Greater Hazleton Historical Society
Website: http://www.hazletonhistory.org

Greater Pittston Historical Society
Website: https://www.facebook.com/GreaterPittstonHistoricalSociety

Huber Breaker Preservation Society
Website: http://www.huberbreaker.org

Luzerne County Historical Society
Website: https://luzernehistory.org

Nanticoke Historical Society
Website: https://nanticokehistoryonline.org

Nathan Denison House
Website: https://luzernehistory.org/visit/denison-house

Northeast Pennsylvania Genealogical Society, Inc.
Website: https://nepgs.com

Plymouth Historical Society
Website: https://www.plymouthhistoricalsocietyluzernecopa.org

***

Lycoming County

Blooming Grove Historical Society
Website: https://www.historicbloominggrove.org

East Lycoming Historical Society
Website: https://www.facebook.com/EastLycomingHistoricalSociety

Jersey Shore Historical Society
Website: https://jshistory.org

Lycoming County Genealogical Society
Website: https://lycominglineage.editorx.io/lycominglineage

Montgomery Area Historical Society
Website: https://www.facebook.com/montgomeryareahistoricalsociety

Muncy Historical Society and Museum of History
Website: http://www.MuncyHistoricalSociety.org

Preservation of Williamsport Foundation, Inc.
Website: https://www.preservationwilliamsport.com/about-pw

Thomas T. Taber Museum
Website: https://tabermuseum.org

***

McKean County

Bradford Landmark Society
Website: http://www.bradfordlandmark.org

Eldred World War II Museum
Website: http://eldredpawwiimuseum.com

Kane Community Depot and Museum
Website: https://www.paroute6.com/the-kane-depot

Penn-Brad Oil Museum
Website: https://penn-bradoilmuseum.org

***

Mercer County

Canal Museum
Website: http://greenvillemuseumalliance.org/canal-museum

Grove City Historical Society
Website: http://www.grovecityhistoricalsociety.org

Hermitage Historical Society
Website:
https://www.hermitage.net/364/Hermitage-Historical-Society

Jamestown Historical Society
Website: https://jamestownhistoricalsociety.org

Mercer County Genealogical Society
Website: https://www.facebook.com/mcgenealogy.pa

Mercer County Historical Society
Website: https://www.facebook.com/MCHSinPA

Sharpsville Historical Society
Website: http://www.sharpsvillehistorical.com/index.htm

***

Mifflin County

Mifflin County Historical Society
Website: https://www.mifflincountyhistory.org/Home.html

Mifflin County Mennonite Historical Society
Website: https://www.facebook.com/p/Mifflin-County-Mennonite-Historical-Society-100032495240977

***

Monroe County

Antoine Dutot Museum and Gallery
Website: https://dutotmuseum.org

Barrett Township Historical Society
Website: https://www.barretthistorical.org

Bell School
Website: https://www.bellschool.com

Historical Association of Tobyhanna Township
Website: http://tobyhannatwphistory.org

Quiet Valley Living Historical Farm
Website: http://www.quietvalley.org

Pocono Indian Museum
Website: https://poconoindianmuseum.com

**

Montgomery County

Amy B. Yerkes Museum
Website: https://www.millbrooksociety.org/museum-collection

Anthracite Railroads Historical Society
Website: https://www.anthraciterailroads.org

Bertolet Meeting House and Burial Ground
Website: https://ccpickell.wixsite.com/bertoletmeetinghouse

Conshohocken Historical Society
Website: https://www.conshohockenhistoricalsociety.org

Goschenhoppen Folklife Library and Museum
Website: https://goschenhoppen.org

Harriton House
Website: https://www.harritonhouse.org

Heckler Plains Folklife Society
Website: https://www.facebook.com/HecklerPlains.org

Highlands Historical Home
Website: https://www.highlandshistorical.org

Historical Society of Fort Washington
Website: http://www.fortwashingtonhistory.org

Historical Society of Montgomery County
Website: http://www.hsmcpa.org

Historic Trappe and Center for Pennsylvania German Studies
Website: https://historictrappe.org

King of Prussia Historical Society
Website: http://www.kophistory.org

Lansdale Historical Society
Website: https://lansdalehistory.org

Limerick Township Historical Society
Website: http://www.limerickpahistory.org

Lower Merion Historical Society
Website: https://lowermerionhistory.org

Lower Pottsgrove Historical Society
Website: http://lowerpottsgrovehistoricalsociety.org/site

Lower Providence Historical Society
Website: https://lphistoricalsociety.webs.com

Mennonite Heritage Center
Website: https://mhep.org

Millbrook Society
Website: https://www.millbrooksociety.org

Montgomery Township Historical Society
Website: http://www.knappfarm.org

Norristown Preservation Society
Website: http://www.norristownpreservationsociety.org

Old York Road Historical Society
Website: http://www.oyrhs.org

Peter Wentz Farmstead Society
Website: https://peterwentzfarmsteadsociety1.org

Plymouth Meeting Historical Society
Website: http://www.plymtghistsoc.freehosting.net

Pottstown Historical Society
Website: http://www.pottstownhistory.org

Saunders House
Website: https://www.saundersnursing.com

Schuylkill Canal Association, Inc.
Website: http://www.schuylkillcanal.com

Schwenkfelder Library and Heritage Center
Website: http://www.schwenkfelder.com

Skippack Historical Society
Website: http://skippack.org/shs.htm

Spring-Ford Area Historical Society
Website: https://www.sfahs.com

Upper Moreland Historical Association
Website: https://uppermorelandhistory.org

Upper Salford Historical Society
Website: https://www.facebook.com/uppersalfordhistory

Welsh Valley Preservation Society
Website: http://www.morganloghouse.org

Wissahickon Valley Historical Society
Website: http://www.wvalleyhs.org

Worcester Historical Society
Website: https://www.facebook.com/WorcesterHistoricalSocietyPA

***

Montour County

Montour County Historical Society
Website: https://montourcountyhistoricalsociety.org

Monroe County

Historical Association of Tobyhanna Township
Website: http://tobyhannatwphistory.org

***

Northampton County

Historic Bethlehem Partnership Museum and Educational Services
Website: http://www.historicbethlehem.org

Easton Area Public Library – Marx Local History Room
Website: https://www.eastonpl.org/MarxRoomHome.html

Easton Heritage Alliance
Website: https://heritageday.org

Hellertown Historical Society
Website: https://www.hellertownhistoricalsociety.org

Hugh Moore National Canal Museum
Website: https://canals.org

Jacobsburg Historical Society
Website: https://www.jacobsburghistory.com

Lehigh Township Historical Society
Website: http://www.lehightownshiphistoricalsociety.org

Lower Saucon Township Historical Society
Website: https://lutzfranklin.wordpress.com

Moravian Historical Society
Website: http://www.moravianhistoricalsociety.org

Moravian Museum of Bethlehem
Website: https://historicbethlehem.org

National Museum of Industrial History
Website: http://www.nmih.org

Northampton County Historical and Genealogical Society
Website: https://sigalmuseum.org

Slate Belt Historical Society
Website: http://slatebeltheritage.net

South Bethlehem Historical Society
Website: https://southbethhistsoc.org

Walnutport Canal Association, Inc.
Website: https://walnutportcanalassociation.tripod.com/index.html

***

NORTHUMBERLAND COUNTY

Mahanoy and Mahantongo Historical Preservation Society
Website: https://www.facebook.com/p/Mahanoy-and-Mahantongo-Historical-Preservation-Society-100067969141483

Milton Historical Society
Website: https://www.miltonpahistoricalsociety.com

Northumberland County Historical Society
Website: https://www.northumberlandcountyhistoricalsociety.org

Warrior Run Church
Website: https://freelandfarm.org/warrior-run-church

***

Perry County

Historical Society of Perry County
Website: http://www.hsofpc.org

Perry Historians
Website: http://www.theperryhistorians.org

***

Philadelphia

Academy of Natural Sciences of Drexel University Library and Archives
Website: https://ansp.org/research/library

ACES Veterans Museum
Website: https://acesveteransmuseum.com

African American Genealogy Group
Website: https://aagg.org

African American Museum of Philadelphia
Website: https://www.aampmuseum.org

American Swedish Historical Museum
Website: https://www.americanswedish.org

Athenaeum of Philadelphia
Website: http://www.philaathenaeum.org

Bridesburg Historical Society
Website: https://www.facebook.com/Bridesburg-Historical-Society-346411578320

Chestnut Hill Conservancy and Historical Society
Website: http://chconservancy.org

Cliveden of the National Trust, Inc.
Website: https://cliveden.org

Eastern State Penitentiary Historic Site
Website: http://www.easternstate.org

Elfreth's Alley Association
Website: http://www.elfrethsalley.org

Frankford Historical Society
Website: https://www.thehistoricalsocietyoffrankford.org

Germantown Mennonite Historic Trust
Website: http://www.meetinghouse.info

Grand Army of the Republic Civil War Museum and Library
Website: http://www.garmuslib.org

Greek American Heritage Museum of Philadelphia
Website: http://gahsp.org

Historical Dental Museum
Website: https://dentistry.temple.edu/about/museum

Historical Society of Tacony
Website: http://www.historictacony.org

Independence Seaport Museum
Website: http://www.phillyseaport.org

Jewish Genealogical Society of Philadelphia
Website: http://www.jewishgen.org/jgsp

Masonic Library and Museum of Pennsylvania
Website: http://www.pagrandlodge.org

Mummers Museum
Website: https://www.mummersmuseum.org

Museum of Nursing History, Inc.
Website: https://nursinghistory.org

Museum of the American Philosophical Society
Website: https://www.amphilsoc.org

Museum of the American Revolution
Website: http://amrevmuseum.org

Mutter Museum
Website: https://muttermuseum.org

National Jewish Museum
Website: https://theweitzman.org

Old Saint Joseph's Historic Preservation Corp
Website: http://www.oldstjoseph.org

Ormiston Mansion
Website: https://www.ormistonmansion.org

Paul Robeson House Museum
Website: https://www.paulrobesonhouse.org

Philadelphia Museum of Art
Website: http://www.philamuseum.org

Polish American Cultural Center Museum
Website: http://www.polishamericancenter.org

Powel House Museum
Website: https://www.philalandmarks.org/powel-house

Rosenbach Museum and Library
Website: https://rosenbach.org

Roxborough Manayunk Wissahickon Historical Society
Website: https://www.rmwhs.org

Science History Institute
Website: https://www.sciencehistory.org/othmer-library

Stenton Museum
Website: https://www.stenton.org

Swedish Colonial Society
Website: https://colonialswedes.net

Temple Judea Museum of Keneseth Israel
Website: https://templejudeamuseum.pastperfectonline.com

Union League of Philadelphia Library Committee
Website: http://www.unionleague.org

University City Historical Society
Website: https://uchs.net

Woodford Mansion
Website: http://www.woodfordmansion.org

Woodlands Mansion and Cemetery
Website: http://www.woodlandsphila.org

Wyck Association
Website: http://www.wyck.org

***

Pike County

Dingmans Ferry-Delaware Township Historical Society
Website: https://dingmansferryhistoricalsociety.org

Gray Towers Heritage Association
Website: https://greytowers.org

National Friends of Grey Towers
Website: https://www.fs.usda.gov/greytowers

Pike County Historical Society
Website: https://www.pikehistorical.org

Shohola Railroad and Historical Society
Website: http://www.wallenpaupackhistorical.org

Wallenpaupack Historical Society
Website: http://www.wallenpaupackhistorical.org

***

POTTER COUNTY

Oswayo Valley Historical Society
Website: https://oswayovalleyhistoricalsociety.com

Pennsylvania Lumber Museum
Website: http://lumbermuseum.org

Potter County Historical Society
Website: https://www.facebook.com/pottercountyhistoricalsociety

***

SCHUYLKILL COUNTY

Ashland Area Historical Preservation Society
Website: https://www.aahps.net

Historical Society of Schuylkill County
Website: http://www.schuylkillhistory.org

Mahanoy Area Historical Society
Website: https://mahanoyhistory.org

Minersville Area Historical Society
Website: https://minershistory.com

Orwigsburg Historical Society
Website: https://www.facebook.com/orwigsburghistory

Railway Restoration Project 113
Website: https://www.rrproject113.org

Saint Clair Historical Society
Website: https://stclairhistoricalsociety.com

Schuylkill Haven Historical Society
Website: https://www.facebook.com/Schuylkill-Haven-Area-Historical-Society-438878806857916

Schuylkill Historical Fire Society
Website: http://www.theshfs.org

Tamaqua Historical Society and Museum
Website: https://www.tamaquahistoricalsociety.org

Tremont Area Historical Society
Website: http://www.tremonthistory.org

***

SNYDER COUNTY

Snyder County Historical Society
Website: http://www.snydercounty.org

***

Somerset County

1901 Church, Inc.
Website: http://www.steeplesproject.org

Berlin Area Historical Society
Website: https://berlinpa.org

Boswell Area Historical Society
Website: http://boswellpa.com

Conemaugh Township Area Historical Society
Website: https://www.facebook.com/ConemaughTownshipAreaHistoricalSociety

Historical and Genealogical Society of Somerset County
Website: http://www.somersethistoricalcenter.org

Hooversville Historical Society
Website: https://pghmuseums.org/directory-content/hooversville-area-historic-society

Meyersdale Area Historical Society
Website: https://www.meyersdaleahs.com

Rockwood Area Historical Society
Website: https://fccrockwood.org/community-services/rockwood-area-historical-society

Quecreek Mine Rescue Foundation
Website: http://quecreekrescue.org

Salisbury-Elk Lick Historical Association
Website: http://www.salisburypa.com

Shade Central Historical Society
Website: http://shadecchs.weebly.com

Springs Historical Society and Museum
Website: http://www.springspa.org

Stoystown Historic District
Website: https://www.livingplaces.com/PA/Somerset_County/Stoystown_Borough/Stoystown_Historic_District.html

***

Sullivan County

Eagles Mere Museum
Website: https://eaglesmeremuseum.com

Endless Mountains War Memorial Museum
Website: https://www.facebook.com/EndlessMountainsWarMemorialMuseum

Sullivan County Historical Society
Website: http://www.scnyhistory.org

***

Susquehanna County

Brooklyn Historical Society
Website: http://brooklynpahistoricalsociety.net

Clifford Township Historical Society
Website: https://cliffordtownshiphistoricalsociety.org

Harford Historical Society
Website:

https://www.facebook.com/Harford-Historical-Society-121858607841961

Old Mill Village Museum
Website: https://oldmillvillage.org

Susquehanna County Historical Society
Website: https://www.susqcohistsoc.org

***

Tioga County

Coates Heritage House Museum
Website: http://www.coates-heritage.iwarp.com

Elkland PA Historical Society
Website: http://www.coates-heritage.iwarp.com

Pennsylvania Historical Association
Website: http://www.pa-history.org

Tioga County Historical Society
Website: https://tiogahistory.org

***

Union County

Mifflinburg Buggy Museum
Website: http://buggymuseum.org

Union County Historical Society
Website: http://unioncountyhistoricalsocietynj.org

Venango County

National Transit Building
Website: http://nationaltransitbuilding.com

Venango County Genealogical Society
Website: https://www.facebook.com/VenangoCountyGenealogicalClub

Venango County Historical Society
Website: http://venango.pa-roots.com

Venango Museum of Art, Science, and Industry
Website: http://www.venangomuseum.org

***

Warren County

Elk Township Historical Society
Website: https://www.facebook.com/ElkTownshipHistoricalSociety

Simpler Times Museum
Website: https://www.facebook.com/Simpler-Times-Museum-2164762166934949

Warren County Historical Society
Website: https://warrenhistory.org

Wilder Museum
Website: https://warrenhistory.org/Wilder%20Museum/wilder_museum.html

***

Washington County

Bradford House Historical Association
Website: https://www.bradfordhouse.org

California Area Historical Society
Website: https://calpahistoricalsociety.org

Charleroi Area Historical Society
Website: https://www.facebook.com/charhistsoc

Donora Historical Society
Website: https://sites.google.com/site/donorahistoricalsociety

Fort Vance Historical Society
Website: http://fortvance.org

Jefferson Township Historical Society
Website: https://jeffersontwphs.com

Meadowcroft Rockshelter and Historic Village
Website: https://www.heinzhistorycenter.org/meadowcroft

Monongahela Area Historical Society
Website: https://mahs-pa.org

Pennsylvania Trolley Museum
Website: https://pa-trolley.org

Peters Creek Historical Society
Website: http://peterscreekhistoricalsociety.org

Washington County Landmarks
Website: http://washcolandmarks.com

***

Wayne County

Equinunk Historical Society
Website: https://www.equinunkhistory.com

Greene-Dreher Historical Society
Website: https://www.greenedreherhs.org

Mount Pleasant Historical Society
Website: https://www.facebook.com/MPAHistoricalSociety

Waymart Area Historical Society
Website: http://www.visitwaynecounty.com/place/waymart_area_historical_society

Wayne County Historical Society
Website: http://www.WayneHistoryPA.org

***

Westmoreland County

Allegheny Township Historical Society
Website: https://www.facebook.com/Allegheny-Township-Historical-Society-113090752428971

Avonmore Area Historical Society
Website: http://avonmorepa.org/history-heritage

Baltzer Meyer Historical Society
Website: https://www.baltzermeyer.com

Bell Township Historic Preservation Society
Website: https://www.bellcountyhistorical.org

Bushy Run Battlefield Heritage Society, Inc.
Website: https://bushyrunbattlefield.com

Delmont Historical Restoration Society
Website: https://delmonthistorical.org

Derry Area Historical Society
Website: http://www.derryhistory.org

Fort Ligonier Association
Website: http://www.fortligonier.org

Greater Monessen Heritage Society
Website: https://monessenhistoricalsociety.com

Greensburg Fire Museum, Inc.
Website: https://gbgfire.com/museum

Latrobe Area Historical Society
Website: https://www.latrobehistory.org

Ligonier Valley Historical Society
Website: https://www.compassinn.org

Norwin Historical Society
Website: https://www.norwinhistoricalsociety.org

Rostraver Township Historical Society
Website: https://www.facebook.com/fellschurch1835

Scottdale Historical Society, Inc.
Website: https://www.scottdalehistoricalsociety.com/about-us

Victorian Vandergrift Museum and Historical Society
Website: https://www.vvmhs.org/

Westmoreland County Historical Society
Website: https://westmorelandhistory.org

Westmoreland Museum of American Art
Website: http://www.wmuseumaa.org

West Overton Village and Museum
Website: http://www.westovertonvillage.org

***

Wyoming County

Wyoming County Historical Society
Website: http://www.pawchs.org

***

York County

Agricultural and Industrial Museum of York County
Website: https://www.yorkhistorycenter.org/york-pa-museums

Dallastown Area Historical Society
Website: https://dallastownhistoricalsociety.org

Fire Museum of York County
Website: https://www.yorkhistorycenter.org/york-pa-museums

Hanover Area Historical Society
Website: https://hahs.us

Indian Steps Museum
Website: https://www.indiansteps.org

Lower Windsor Area Historical Society
Website: https://www.facebook.com/LowerWindsorAreaHistoricalSociety

Neas House Museum
Website: https://mainstreethanover.org/neas-house

Wirt Park Fire Station Museum
Website: https://iaff2045.com/stations/station-79-1-wirt-park

Kreutz Creek Valley Preservation Society
Website: https://sites.google.com/site/kcvpsociety

Manheim Fire Company Museum
Website: http://www.manheimfire.com/museum.htm

Maryland and Pennsylvania Railroad Preservation Society
Website: http://www.maandparailroad.com

New Oxford Area Historical Society
Website: https://www.facebook.com/NOAHS17350

Northern York County Historical and Preservation Society
Website: http://www.northernyorkhistorical.org

Old Line Museum
Website: https://www.facebook.com/oldlinemuseum

Police Heritage Museum
Website: http://www.policeheritagemuseum.com

Red Lion Area Historical Society
Website: http://redlionareahistoricalsociety.org

South Central Pennsylvania Genealogical Society
Website: https://www.scpgs.org

Spring Grove Area Historical Society
Website: https://sgahps.org

Stewartstown Historical Society
Website: http://stewhist.org/

Wellsville Area Historical Society
Website: https://www.facebook.com/WellsvilleHistory

West Manchester Historical Society
Website: https://www.facebook.com/westmanchestertwphistoricalsoc/

Wrightsville Historical Museum
Website: https://www.historicwrightsvillepa.org/wrightsville-historic

York County History Center
Website: https://www.yorkhistorycenter.org

Chapter 10

Federal and State Historical Sites

IT CAN SEEM UNUSUAL to list historical sites for genealogy research; however, if you know the history of a place, you learn about the people too.

The historical sites listed below are managed by either the Pennsylvania Historical and Museum Commission (PHMC) or the National Park Service (NPS). These sires are supported by government tax dollars for maintenance and staffing, supplemented by entrance or activity fees. You will find that each location also has a research library, archival materials, and deeply knowledgeable staff to help you advance your research. Some historical sites have digitized or indexed their materials, and you'll find this under website pages titled "Research". You can also contact the site via their webpage for assistance.

The PHMC also manages the State Museum of Pennsylvania, located on the state capitol complex and covering all Pennsylvania's history. Their website is https://statemuseumpa.org.

If you have the opportunity to visit historic sites relevant to the time or place you are researching, you will walk away with contextual information that cannot be gained through internet research. Standing in the place where history happened that brings the past to life in a way nothing else can.

The sites here are grouped by topic, not location. If a location covers more than one topic, it is listed under each one.

***

Colonial Heritage

Re-creations of Pennsylvania's early history, focusing on settlement, governance, and colonial life.

Cornwall Iron Furnace
Website: https://www.cornwallironfurnace.org

Eckley Miners' Village
Website: https://eckleyminersvillage.com

Ephrata Cloister
Website: https://ephratacloister.org

Fort Necessity National Battlefield
Website: https://www.nps.gov/fone

Friendship Hill National Historic Site
Website: https://www.nps.gov/frhi

Graeme Park
Website: https://www.graemepark.org

Hope Lodge
Website: https://www.historichopelodge.org

Hopewell Furnace National Historic Site
Website: https://www.nps.gov/hofu

Independence National Historical Park
Website: https://www.nps.gov/inde

Landis Valley Village & Farm Museum
Website: https://www.landisvalleymuseum.org

Old Economy Village
Website: https://oldeconomyvillage.org

Pennsbury Manor
Website: https://www.pennsburymanor.org

Thaddeus Kosciuszko National Memorial
Website: https://www.nps.gov/thko

Valley Forge National Historical Park
Website: https://www.nps.gov/vafo

***

Military History

These sites explore Pennsylvania's pivotal role in military conflicts, from colonial times to modern wars.

Brandywine Battlefield Park
Website: https://www.brandywinebattlefield.org

Bushy Run Battlefield
Website: https://bushyrunbattlefield.com

Conrad Weiser Homestead
Website: https://www.conradweiserhomestead.org

Cornwall Iron Furnace
Website: https://www.cornwallironfurnace.org

Daniel Boone Homestead
Website: https://www.danielboonehomestead.org

Eisenhower National Historic Site
Website: https://www.nps.gov/eise/index.htm

Erie Maritime Museum and U.S. Brig Niagara
Website: https://www.eriemaritimemuseum.org

Fort Pitt Museum
Website: https://www.heinzhistorycenter.org/fort-pitt

Gettysburg National Military Park
Website: https://www.nps.gov/gett/learn/historyculture

Pennsylvania Military Museum
Website: https://www.pamilmuseum.org

Washington Crossing Historic Park
Website: https://www.washingtoncrossingpark.org

***

Industrial Heritage and Innovation

These locastions focus on Pennsylvania's industrial past, showcasing sites related to mining, ironmaking, railroads, and oil production.

Allegheny Portage Railroad National Historic Site
Website: https://www.nps.gov/alpo

Cornwall Iron Furnace
Website: https://www.cornwallironfurnace.org

Drake Well Museum and Park
Website: https://www.drakewell.org

Hopewell Furnace National Historic Site
Website: https://www.nps.gov/hofu

Johnstown Flood National Memorial
Website: https://www.nps.gov/jofl

Joseph Priestley House
Website: https://www.josephpriestleyhouse.org

Pennsylvania Lumber Museum
Website: https://lumbermuseum.org

Pennsylvania Anthracite Heritage Museum
Website: https://www.anthracitemuseum.org

Pennsylvania Lumber Museum
Website: https://lumbermuseum.org

Railroad Museum of Pennsylvania
Website: https://www.rrmuseumpa.org

Scranton Iron Furnaces
Website: https://www.anthracitemuseum.org/scranton-iron-furnaces

Steamtown National Historic Site
Website: https://www.nps.gov/stea

***

RELIGIOUS AND MEMORIAL SITES

These places were founded by religious groups significant to the state's history or mark the site of a tragic deaths.

Ephrata Cloister
Website: https://ephratacloister.org

Flight 93 National Memorial
Website: https://www.nps.gov/flni

Johnstown Flood National Memorial
Website: https://www.nps.gov/jofl

Old Economy Village
Website: https://oldeconomyvillage.org

Chapter 11

Religious Organization Archives

No AMERICAN COLONY HAD more religious groups than Pennsylvania.

By the time of the Revolutionary War, the state had dozens of distinct faiths practiced by its citizens. By 1860, on the eve of the Civil War, there were dozens more as existing denominations split over the question of slavery. Pennsylvania was also home to unique religious groups who lived communally and practiced their faith.

All of these factors make genealogy research in religious records a challenge.

Adding to this research challenge is determining where historical records of congregations are currently stored. Congregational records could be kept locally, regionally, or nationally by a denomination. In some cases, the denomination does not have the records at all; instead, they may be found in a local archive, such as a historical society or university special collections library. In other cases, a church has changed its name and/or location many times and researchers have to reconstruct its history to the proper name. Some historical religious records for some years for some locations have been microfilmed and made available online, but online collections are never complete. It takes considerable time and patience to be thorough in religious record research.

If the religion of an ancestor is unknown, start by listing the religious congregations within 20 miles of the ancestor's location. Use a map and note the denominations and the name of each of the congregations. Once you have this list, church record collections on genealogy websites can be searched to see if one of your listed congregations is there. If not, often the local county genealogical or historical society has copies or transcriptions for the historical congregations in their area. After these two searches are completed, a further search can be made at the denominations' main archives listed below.

The main office or headquarters of a religious organization may hold additional records on its members. Examples of additional records include: ancestors who violated the religion's norms, those who transferred out or into the faith, and individuals who served as leaders, ministers, or missionaries.

To repeat: no religious denomination has a fully complete, indexed collection of historical records available online. There are always missing years, missing locations, and missing pages within records. To conduct thorough research, research must be conducted in the archival records of the religious organization and locally in genealogical and historical societies.

Religious faiths which began in Pennsylvania prior to 1920 are listed below, since the majority of traditional genealogy research occurs prior to 20th century. The foundation date listed for the faith is the year it began in Pennsylvania (Many faiths go back hundreds to thousands of years prior to arrival in the state). An excellent book to understand the tenets of each of the faiths listed below is the *Handbook of Denominations in the United States*. It is regularly updated to include newly organized, or re-organized, religions.

Helpful resource: If you have colonial residents of Philadelphia in your family tree, many of these historical religious records are free to access from home. Philadelphia's earliest congregations of all faiths have digitized their records and published them on *Philadelphia Congregations Early Records*, website at **https://philadelphiacongregations.org/records** .

***

ANABAPTISTS (SEPARATISTS UNAFFILIATED)

In 1517 after the Reformation, several Anabaptist groups formed in Switzerland, Germany, and France. These groups include the Amish, Brethren, German Reformed, Harmony Society, Mennonites, Moravians, and Schwenkfelders – all iconic in Pennsylvania culture. Each of these Anabaptist groups has distinct dress and cultural practices causing them to stand out in modern society. They are called Anabaptists for their common practice of denying the validity of infant baptism. They only accept and practice adult baptism. These Anabaptist faiths are also known as Separatists Unaffiliated in some research archives. See each group's separate listing below.

***

ADVENTISTS

This religious movement began in the mid-1800s and focused on the return of Christ as Biblical prophecy. They were seen as dangerous radicals at the time and had relatively small congregations. There is no central archive of Pennsylvania followers and there are several distinct churches within adventism.

Advent Christian Church General Conference
Founded: 1860
Website: https://www.acgc.us

Christadelphian
Founded: 1844
Website: http://christadelphia.org

Church of God (Seventh Day)
Founded: 1863
Website: https://cog7.org

Church of God and Saints in Christ (Black Hebrew Israelites)
Founded: 1896
Website: https://cogasoc.net

Jehovah's Witness (Watch Tower Bible and Tract Society)
Founded: 1870
Website: https://www.jw.org

Seventh-Day Adventist
Founded: 1863
Website: https://www.adventist.org

***

Amish

There is no central repository of Amish church records. Each Amish sect maintains its own membership records back to its founding. The way to determine if an ancestor was Amish would be in family lore or newspaper articles. Deaths of Amish community members are not reported in newspaper obituaries.

***

Baptist

The Baptist movement grew out of the Puritan faith in New England and the Anabaptist faith in Pennsylvania. It become popular in the 1740s and developed regional differences as it spread. The formation date of the church in American is considered 1814 when the various congregations met in Philadelphia. The listings below are Baptist groups which formed in Pennsylvania. There are dozens more groups that formed across the US. A majority of black people prior to the Civil War were Baptist or Methodist.

American Baptist Churches in the USA
Founded: 1814
Website: https://www.abc-usa.org

National Baptist Convention of America
Founded: 1895
Website: https://nationalbaptist.com

North American Baptist Conference
Founded: 1865
Website: https://nabconference.org

Seventh Day Baptist General Conference
Founded: 1802, with roots to 1700
Website: https://www.seventhdaybaptist.org

***

Brethren

The Brethren faith was formed out of the Pietist movement in the Lutheran church in late 1600s Germany. They are part of the Anabaptist faiths and lived near those of other Anabaptist faiths, so check the organizations listed under those faiths too. National headquarters listed below may also assist in historical record searches.

Brethren in Christ
Founded: 1863, with roots to 1760s
Website: https://bicus.org

Church of the Brethren
Founded: 1708
Website: https://www.brethren.org

Church of the United Brethren in Christ
Founded: 1800, with roots to 1767
Website: https://ub.org

Evangelical Congregational Church
Founded: 1894, with roots to 1800
Website: https://eccenter.com

***

Catholic (Orthodox)

The Orthodox Catholic faith arrived in Pennsylvania around the beginning of the 20th century. Different ethnic groups – Greek, Russian, Ukrainian – each founded their own churches in their communities. Researchers should first contact the church itself in the ancestral community first, then each church's organizing office listed below.

Byzantine Catholic Archeparchy of Pittsburgh
Website: https://www.archpitt.org

Orthodox Church in America (Russian Orthodox)
Founded: 1897
Website: https://www.oca.org/history-archives

Ukrainian Catholic Archeparchy of Philadelphia
Founded: 1924
Website: http://ukrarcheparchy.us

***

Catholic (Roman)

Roman Catholic and Orthodox Catholic church records are held in regional diocese archives or locally by the congregation. Contact the diocese to determine their record holdings.

Archdiocese of Philadelphia, Catholic Historical Research Center
Counties: Bucks, Chester, Delaware, Montgomery, and Philadelphia
Website: https://chrc-phila.org

Diocese of Allentown
Counties: Berks, Carbon, Lehigh, Northampton, and Schuylkill
Website: https://www.allentowndiocese.org

Diocese of Altoona-Johnstown
Counties: Bedford, Blair, Cambria, Centre, Clinton, Fulton, Huntingdon, and Somerset
Website: https://www.dioceseaj.org

Diocese of Erie, Saint Mark Center
Counties: Cameron, Clarion, Clearfield, Crawford, Elk, Erie, Forest, Jefferson, McKean, Mercer, Potter, Venango, and Warren
Website: https://www.eriercd.org

Diocese of Greensburg
Counties: Armstrong, Fayette, Indiana, and Westmoreland
Website: https://ww.dioceseofgreensburg.org

Diocese of Pittsburgh, Cardinal Dearden Center
Counties: Allegheny, Beaver, Butler, Greene, Lawrence, Washington
Website: https://www.diopitt.org

Diocese of Scranton
Counties: Bradford, Lackawanna, Luzerne, Lycoming, Monroe, Pike, Sullivan, Susquehanna, Tioga, Wayne and Wyoming
Website: https://www.dioceseofscranton.org

***

EPISCOPAL

People of Episcopal faith arrived soon after the Quakers in Pennsylvania. Like with most religions, the church began in

Philadelphia, then spread from there. Historical records for all Episcopal churches in the state are held in Philadelphia. The one exception is the African Episcopal Church of St. Thomas which maintains its own archive.

Diocese of Pennsylvania
Founded: 1695
Website: https://www.diopa.org

African Episcopal Church of St. Thomas Archive
Founded: 1792
Website: http://www.aecst.org/archives.htm

***

Holiness

The Holiness movement grew out of the Methodist church in the 19th century. It is similar to the Pentecostal faith encouraging a personal relationship with the Holy Spirit. Many of the faiths below appealed to new immigrants to the US, clustered in tenement city housing. Historical church records could be found with the church itself or the national office.

Apostolic Christian Churches of America
Founded: 1840s
Website: https://www.apostolicchristian.org

The Christian and Missionary Alliance
Founded: 1887
Website: https://cmalliance.org

Church of the Nazarene
Founded: 1908
Website: https://nazarene.org

The Salvation Army
Founded: 1880
Website: https://www.salvationarmyusa.org

Wesleyan Church
Founded: 1968, with roots to 1843
Website: https://www.wesleyan.org

***

Jewish

The Jewish faith was practiced early in the history of the colony of Pennsylvania. Early records are dispersed across three PA archives, each holding historical synagogue and cemetery records, local Jewish newspapers, and family papers and histories. Key repositories for historical Jewish records include:

Rauh Jewish History Program & Archives
Heinz History Center
Website:
https://www.heinzhistorycenter.org/collections/rauh-jewish-history-program-and-archives

Historical Society of Pennsylvania
Website:
https://hsp.org/collections/catalogs-research-tools/subject-guides/jewish-resources

Philadelphia Jewish Archives Collection
Special Collections Research Center (SCRC), Temple University Libraries
Website:
https://library.temple.edu/collections/philadelphia-jewish-archives-collection

***

Latter Day Saints

The Church of Jesus Christ of Latter-day Saints (LDS), also known as the Mormon Church, and the Church of Jesus Christ, is well-known to genealogists. The LDS church requires members to research and document at least four generations of family history. To assist members in this requirement the Utah Genealogical Association microfilmed millions of records around the US beginning in the 1950s. These collected records became FamilySearch.

The Church of Jesus Christ of Latter-Day Saints
Founded: 1830
Website: https://www.churchofjesuschrist.org

***

Lutheran

The Lutheran church is one of the largest religious faiths in the country and is known today as the Evangelical Lutheran Church in America. There are also regional variations of the faith across the country. Start by checking with local genealogical and historical societies in your ancestors' county before contacting these regional and national archives. Ancestry has a digitization agreement with the Lutheran Archives Center in Philadelphia to image the oldest American records.

Evangelical Lutheran Church in America
Founded: 1748
Website: https://www.elca.org

Eastern Pennsylvania (and All Records Older than 1840) Lutheran Archives Center at Philadelphia
Website: http://www.lacphila.org

Western Pennsylvania
Sarah (Sally) Roth Tri-Synod Archives, Thiel College
Website: https://www.thiel.edu/library/the-thiel-archives

Central Pennsylvania
A.R. Wentz Library, United Lutheran Seminary
Website: http://library.uls.edu/subjects/guide.php?subject=archives

National Archives
Evangelical Lutheran Church in America Archives
Website: https://www.elca.org/archives

***

MENNONITE

There are two distinct groups of Mennonites: "Old Order" Mennonites which follow the Anabaptist traditions described above, and the contemporary Mennonite church which looks like most Christian churches. Below is listed the Mennonite headquarters as well as three local historical societies with their records. Mennonites were pacifists and did not participate in the militia or military. The organizations below provide a good starting place for research of members.

Mennonite Church USA
Founded: 1683
Website: https://www.mennoniteusa.org

Juniata Mennonite Historical Center
Website: http://www.juniatamennonitehistoricalcenter.com

Mennonite Heritage Center
Website: https://mhep.org/

Mennonite Life (formerly The Mennonite Historical Society)
Website: https://mennonitelife.org

Methodist

The Methodist faith developed out of the Church of England in the 1730s. Methodism spread rapidly across the US, converting many Presbyterians, Episcopalians, and Lutherans. Most historical congregational records are kept by the churches themselves, if the church is still in operation. Closed churches send their records to the archives listed below. Prior to the Civil War, many African Americans were either Baptist or Methodist, including African Methodist Episcopal (AME) Church.

African Methodist Episcopal Church
Founded: 1814
Website: https://www.ame-church.com

United Methodist Church
Founded: 1968, with roots to 1784
Website: https://www.umc.org

UMC General Commission on Archives and History
Website: http://gcah.org

***

Moravian

The first Moravians came to Pennsylvania in 1735. Many religious scholars group the Moravian faith with the Brethren faith. The Archives of the Moravian Church has indexed the church registers of their congregations. They are available to search on its website for no charge. The Moravian Historical Society publishes the history of the church community and holds events and exhibitions.

Moravian Church in America
Founded: 1722
Website: https://www.moravian.org

Archives of the Moravian Church
Website: https://www.moravianchurcharchives.org

Moravian Historical Society
Website: https://www.moravianhistory.org

***

PENTECOSTAL

The Pentecostal faith begins in the 20th century, growing out of the Holiness movement (see the Holiness section above for details). A defining characteristic of this religion is the speaking in tongues during services. Since most Pentecostal churches are relatively new, historical records are maintained locally by individual congregations. Historical records are not available online.

Assemblies of God
Founded: 1914
Website: https://ag.org

Church of God in Christ
Founded: 1897
Website: https://www.cogic.org

Pentecostal Assemblies of the World
Founded: 1907
Website: https://pawinc.org

***

Presbyterian

The Scots Irish from Ulster, Ireland were the first Presbyterians in Pennsylvania. The Presbyterian Historical Society has a helpful congregation locator Hall's Index of American Presbyterian Congregations, on its website. The historical society is a repository for church records of closed churches, presbyteries, and synods.

Presbyterian Church USA
Founded: 1680s
Website: https://www.pcusa.org

Presbyterian Historical Society
Website: https://www.history.pcusa.org

***

Quakers (Religious Society of Friends)

Pennsylvania was founded by Quakers in 1681 and was a majority of the population until the Scots Irish and Germans began arriving in the 1730s. There were several schisms in the Quaker faith in the lead up to the Revolutionary War, so careful tracking is necessary. William Wade Hinshaw's six-volume index, *Encyclopedia of American Quaker Genealogy*, published in 1991 is considered the definitive compilation to the Quaker records. The records Hinshaw used for his books and additional Quaker genealogical records are maintained in suburban Philadelphia at Swarthmore College.

Friends Historical Library at Swarthmore College
Website:
https://www.swarthmore.edu/friends-historical-library

***

Reformed (Dutch)

The first Europeans to Pennsylvania were Swedish and Dutch, and most practiced the Reformed faith. A smaller faith in total numbers compared to others in the colonial era. Records of congregations have been archived and many digitized by the New Brunswick Theological Seminary.

New Brunswick Theological Seminary
Reformed Church in America
Website: https://www.rca.org/about/history/archives

***

Reformed (German)

The original records of the German Reformed Church and the Evangelical and Reformed Church are housed at the Lancaster Theological Seminary. Many local historical and genealogical societies also have copies of transcribed records, German to English, which are easier to work with. Many church members were involved in the American Revolution.

Evangelical and Reformed Historical Society
Philip Schaff Library Lancaster Theological Seminary
Website: https://www.lancasterseminary.edu

***

Schwenkfelder

This faith is similar to other Anabaptist faiths and began under the leadership of Caspar Schwenkfeld. The first Schwenkfelders arrived in

Pennsylvania in 1731 and 1737 and settled between Philadelphia and Allentown.

Schwenkfelder Library and Heritage Center
Founded: 1731
Website: https://www.schwenkfelder.org

***

Swedenborgian (The New Church)

The Swedenborgian faith is known as The New Church today. The older membership records of The New Church are maintained at the Bryn Athyn College Library. No genealogical research services offered, but most of the collection is digitized and available on the Swedenborg Library for no charge.

Bryn Athyn College, Swedenborg Library
Website:

https://brynathyn.edu/swedenborg-library/new-church-digital-collections

***

Unitarian and Universalist

The Unitarian faith began in New England Congregational churches and followers were known as "Free Thinkers". The Universalist faith grew out of resistance to the Calvinist idea of pre-determination. The tenets of Universalism were drafted in 1790 in Philadelphia and several congregations sprung up in Erie, Indiana County, and Mercer County. In 1961, the Unitarian and Universalist faiths merged.

The Andover-Harvard Theological Library at Harvard Divinity School is the main repository for Unitarian and Universalist records nationally; however, they have no early records of the Pennsylvania congregations. A listing of congregational records collected and its location is on the Unitarian and Universalist History and Heritage Society website. Some early church records are at the Historical Society of Pennsylvania and the Heinz History Center, as well at the First Unitarian Church of Philadelphia.

The Unitarian and Universalist History and Heritage Society
Website: https://uuhhs.org

First Unitarian Church of Philadelphia
Founded: 1796
Website: https://philauu.org

***

United Church of Christ

The United Church of Christ (UCC) was formally founded in 1957, but has roots to early Congregational and Presbyterian churches. The UCC governing structure is similar to those faiths with councils and synods. Today it is seen as most of the most liberal Christian faiths and shares few of the tenets of its historical roots. Genealogists who find ancestors in this faith will need to search locally for records with the churches themselves. At this time there is not a national or regional archive of historical records.

United Church of Christ
Founded: 1957, with roots to the colonial period
Website: https://www.ucc.org

***

Communal Religious Groups

Pennsylvania's infamous tolerance for any religious practice brought many unique leaders and groups to the colony and state.

The three groups listed below are some of the larger and more well-known religious organizations which operated as communes. There were many other preachers, pastors, and zealots who lived for at least some time in Pennsylvania where they would find followers and then move to another state. For more information on communal religious groups, consult county history books, local historical societies, and regional archives.

Society of the Woman in the Wilderness

This communal group was also formally known as the Content of the God-Loving Soul, and the Chapter of Perfection. These formal names were passed over for its popular name, Society of the Woman in the Wilderness, because of the reference to the Book of Revelation reflected the zeitgeist of the early Pennsylvania colony. There were 40 members led by Johannes Kelpius (1673–ca.1708), and they spent their days in private meditation and study. The group ended when its members passed away.

Some historical materials of the Society's members, meetings, hymnals, and beliefs are in the Abraham H. Cassel collection at the Historical Society of Pennsylvania: http://www2.hsp.org/collections/manuscripts/c/Cassel1610.html

Ephrata Cloister (Seventh Day German Baptist Brethren)

Founded the 1720s, soon after the dissolution of the Society of the Woman in the Wilderness, this communal group was located just east of the city of Lancaster. Members followed a highly regimented daily routine, similar to monastic life of medieval Europe. Ephrata spun off many other colonies in Pennsylvania including: Antietam in Franklin County; Bermudian Creek in York County; and Stony Creek in Somerset County. Founder Conrad Beissel (1697–1768) was closely tied to the Pietist faith in Heidelberg, Germany.

Ephrata Cloister is now a state historical site and records can be found at The Pennsylvania State Archives, website: https://ephratacloister.org

Harmony Society (Rappists)

Founded in the 1790s by Separatists from the Evangelical Lutheran Church, this communal group selected a site in Butler County for their community in 1805. Leader George Rapp (1757–1834) stayed at the original site for only 10 years before leading his people to Indiana in 1814. They returned to Pennsylvania in 1824 and founded Economy Village in Beaver County. It was here that the group awaited the events of the Book of Revelation to play out. The Society formally dissolved in 1916.

The site is managed by the PHMC and records can be found at both The Pennsylvania State Archives and the Old Economy Village website: http://oldeconomyvillage.org. Descendants of the members of Harmony Society hold a reunion each year at Old Economy Village.

Chapter 12

Wrapping Up and Saving Your Research

You did it! You found something in an archive related to your ancestor and you want to keep it for your family history. How exactly do you do that?

Take Digital Images

Digital images are your best option. Many archives now provide scanners onsite for patrons, and staff are often available to assist you in creating clear images and saving them to a USB drive. Some archives may also allow you to bring your own scanner to connect to your laptop—always check requirements before your visit.

However, you don't necessarily need a scanner to produce high-quality images. Modern mobile phones and tablets (especially those made after 2020) create sharper images than 99% of those available on microfilm. Most archives allow researchers to take digital images using mobile devices, as long as no flash is used. For steadier images and even lighting, you can purchase a stand to hold your phone.

Tips for Capturing Images:

- Test Before You Go: Download and practice using scanning apps for iOS or Android well in advance. Most apps offer free trial periods.

- Large Files: If you're scanning a large file—like a Union Army pension file that can include 100-300 pages—pause periodically to ensure that each image is clear and in-frame.

- Separate Record Sets: Between record sets, take a photo of a blank piece of paper, a box label, or a file folder. This creates a clear visual divider on your camera roll.

- Image Settings: Use the highest quality setting your mobile device allows. High-resolution images enable you to zoom in later without losing clarity.

Beware of Copyright

Archival records generally fall into two categories: public records (created by governments) and private records (created by individuals or organizations like businesses, churches, or clubs). Understanding the distinction is key to determining your ability to share or publish these materials.

Public Records

- Original public records (such as land deeds, court records, and military pensions) are free from copyright restrictions.

- **Important Note**: If you download a public record image from a genealogy website like Ancestry or FamilySearch, the image itself is copyrighted by that publisher. While you can use these downloads for personal research, you must check the website's terms of service before sharing or publishing them.

Private Records

- Copyright rules vary widely for private records. Many archives allow digital images for personal use, but sharing or publishing requires verification.

- If you plan to use images on a blog, in a self-published book, or in a YouTube video—even for free—you need explicit permission from the archive. Ideally, this confirmation should be in writing through email or a letter on official letterhead specifying what images you can use and in what ways.

- Fees for Publication: Some archives charge fees for publishing images. Small personal uses (like family blogs or books) may incur minor fees, while larger uses (like commercially published books or paid lectures) may have higher costs.

Helpful Resource: The Society of American Archivists provides a detailed Q&A on copyright and unpublished materials: https://www2.archivists.org/publications/brochures/copyright-and-unpublished-material.

Organize and Back-Up

Genealogists today are drowning in digital images. For over two decades we have been downloading any record we want with a couple of clicks. Now we have hard drives full of images of records of our ancestors. But can we find the record we want when we need it on our computer? Organization is key to not drowning in your own research.

Name your digital images in a way that you can find it again. At a minimum, include the following in your file names:

1. Ancestor's full name

2. Date of the record

3. Type of record

4. Location

By naming files with the surname first, they will sort alphabetically in my downloads folder. When I move the files to my genealogy research folders by family, I can easily scan down the list of file names and see which records belong to each ancestor. I put the the date immediately after the name, so I have a timeline of events in my folder for each individual. Here are some examples:

- Church baptism: Streibig Casper_1834_Baptism_St Mary

Manayunk

- Census: Streibig Casper_1860_Census
- Military pension file: Streibig Casper_1877_ Pension File_NARA

Backing up your personal research files means at least two copies of your computer files, with one being away from your home. Online continual back-ups are ideal, so nothing is lost due to a power surge, system failure, or ransomware attack. Leaving a copy of all your research with other family members is also helpful in case of total disaster such as fire or flood. The simplest way to do this is a USB thumb drive. Encourage those family members to load the research onto their own computers. They may just get interested in your research!

A Few Final Thoughts

My intention with this book is to help you to stretch outside your comfort zone for genealogy research and confidently explore archival research. No one person is an expert in every archive, and even archivists are not experts in every collection within their care. The volume of saved history stored in archives is too much for any one person to master.

You will develop your own habits and methods for archival research as you find valuable collections for genealogy research. As you research and find collections that answer family history questions, please email me at **hello@paancestors.com** and share what you found. I would love to celebrate what you found with you!

As you explore our 340 years of history in the Keystone state, I'll be cheering you on every step of the way. I can not wait to hear about the stories you uncover!

Terms Used by Archives

EVERY PROFESSION HAS SPECIAL vocabulary. Here are the ones you will find used by archives.

ArchiveGrid: A database of over 7 million collection descriptions from archive catalogs, representing a small sample of what is available. Located at: https://researchworks.oclc.org/archivegrid/.

Archives: A repository of preserved historical records of all types. Archives may be public or private, in physical form or digital form or both.

Catalog: A complete listing of items in an archive arranged systematically. Most catalogs of archives are samplings of available records, and not a complete inventory.

Corporate archive: A department within a company or corporation that preserves the history of the organization and its employees. When corporations merge or acquire other companies, the archives usually transfer to the parent corporation or be donated to an institution near the corporate headquarters.

Database: A set of records, usually all related to one source, indexed for searching. Databases can be only text, or text plus images of records.

Diary: A written record of events or personal observations made daily or at regular intervals. Sometimes used interchangeably with "journal".

Digital collections: Images of archival materials usually hosted on a website. In most cases, what is digital also exists in original paper form too. Some materials today are "born digital", such as posts on social media or emails, and did not begin in physical form.

Digitize (digitization): The process of turning physical documents into digital images. To keyword search digitized images, requires indexing (see below).

Document (n and v): As a noun, writing on paper. As a verb, the act of writing on paper.

Family Papers: A collection of personal documents usually for one individual and his or her immediate family. Typically includes letters, diaries, journals, and receipts.

Finding Aid: A document detailing the contents of an archival collection. The descriptions provided are usually by container (box or folder) and broad in nature. Sometimes there are narrative sections providing the historical context of the collection and how the archives acquired it.

FOIA: Acronym for Freedom of Information Act. Applies to requests to federal agencies for release of documents. State agencies have a similar request process that varies by state.

Government archive: A building separate from the regular government offices designed to store materials according to that government's archival policy. All levels of government – federal, state, county, and municipal – have an archive to store records and save space in offices.

Historical societies: Non-profit organizations often staffed by volunteers who seek to preserve and promote the history of a specific region, person, or event.

Image: A digital reproduction of a physical object. In genealogy, this is usually documents, but it can also be photographs, maps, artwork, and three dimensional objects, such as household items, business equipment, and military gear.

Indexing: The process of building a database using the metadata attached to digital images. Once images are indexed into a database they are searchable with keywords by computer programs.

Journal: A regular recording of events of current interest. Sometimes used interchangeably with "diary".

Ledger: A written record of transactions or events made at regular intervals, usually daily.

Manuscript: A handwritten or typewritten document. In archives, manuscripts are unpublished works, as compared to books which are published works.

Microfiche: A sheet of microfilm the size of an index card containing rows of images of documents.

Microfilm: A film roll containing images of documents. The most popular form of preservation for government records.

Museum: A building which exhibits art and artifacts. Sometimes museums also store books and papers related to artists, artwork, and/or the local area where they are located.

Processing: The name for organizing a newly donated collection to an archive. During processing, a finding aid and/or catalog entry is created, and the materials are sorted in folders and boxes for storage.

Public records: Records created by government department and agencies. Public records are by default open for anyone for research, unless restricted for privacy reasons. Public records do not require a FOIA request (see above).

Published: An written document or image, created by one or many individuals, and released for distribution physically or digitally. The creators of published works own the copyright for what they publish, no matter if it is digital or physical.

Record (n and v): As a verb, to set down in writing. As a noun, a document noting events in detail for official purposes.

Religious archives: Also commonly called "church archives". A place which stores the records of a religious denomination collected from around a specific region or the entire country. Example: The Presbyterian Historical Society collects historical membership records from all its churches in the United States.

Restricted collection: Archival material that is limited in use due to content, age, or condition of materials. Each archive sets its own policy for restrictions.

Special collections: The part of a library collection that holds rare and valuable manuscripts, books, and papers. These are often of historical value to the local region around the library.

WorldCat: An internet-based catalog of library materials, located at: https://search.worldcat.org.

Sources

THE FOLLOWING SOURCES WERE used in creation of this book.

Dructor, Robert M., *Guide to Genealogical Sources at the Pennsylvania State Archives, 2nd ed*. Harrisburg: Pennsylvania Historical and Museum Commission, 1998.

Olson, Roger E.; Mead, Frank S.; Hill, Samuel S.; and Atwood. Craig D.; *Handbook of Denominations in the United States, 14th ed.*, Nashville: Abingdon Press, 2018.

Pennsylvania Genealogical Map of the Counties, 11th ed. Harrisburg: Pennsylvania Historical and Museum Commission, 1999.

Pfeiffer, Laura Szucs, *Hidden Sources: Family History in Unlikely Places.* Orem, Utah: Ancestry Publishing, 2000.

Pitzer, Donald E., ed., *America's Communal Utopias*, Chapel Hill: University of North Carolina Press, 1997.

Schmidt, Laura, "Using Archives: A Guide to Effective Research," *Society of American Archivists* (https://www2.archivists.org/usingarchives).

Szucs, Loretto Dennis, and Luebking, Sandra Hargreaves, editors, *The Source: A Guidebook to American Genealogy*, 3rd ed. Provo, Utah: Ancestry, 2006.

Resources to Improve Research Skills

The following books and websites can help with learning name variations, ethnicity of surnames, abbreviations used in original records, location names, and handwriting styles.

Behind the Name, https://surnames.behindthename.com.

Bell, Robert, *The Book of Ulster Surnames*, Ulster Historical Foundation, 2021.

British Surnames, https://britishsurnames.co.uk.

Foreign Versions, Variations, and Diminutives of English Names; Foreign Equivalents of United States Military and Civilian Titles, U.S. Department of Justice, Immigration and Naturalization Service, 1973.

Geogen v4, (German surnames), http://geogen.stoepel.net.

Gordon, Thomas F., *A Gazetteer of the State of Pennsylvania (1832)*, Apollo, PA: Closson Press, 1999.

Guild of One Name Studies, https://one-name.org.

Rose, Christine, *Nicknames Past and Present, 5th ed.*, San Jose, California: CR Publications, 2007.

Sperry, Kip, *Reading Early American Handwriting*, Baltimore: Genealogical Publishing Co., 1998.

Sperry, Kip, *Abbreviations & Acronyms: A Guide for Family Historians, 2nd ed.*, Provo, Utah: Ancestry, 2003.

About the Author

DENYSE ALLEN IS A genealogist on a mission to help you uncover the history of your Pennsylvania ancestors. In 2019, she founded PA Ancestors to provide the resource she wished she had when she began her own genealogical journey.

With a commitment to discovering her eight generations of Pennsylvania ancestors, Denyse has researched their lives in the courthouses and archives of Berks, Blair, Centre, Chester, Clearfield, Dauphin, Delaware, Lancaster, Montgomery, Northampton, Philadelphia, Schuylkill, Snyder, Union, and York counties. She approaches each research trip with a combination of curiosity and daring in search of new records for genealogy. Her experiences are captured in this book, so others can experience the thrill of discovery too.

Denyse's first book is *Pennsylvania Vital Records Research: A Genealogy Guide to Birth, Adoption, Marriage, Divorce, and Death Records from the Colonial Era to Today.* This is her second book.

Free introduction to Pennsylvania genealogy course: https://welcome.paancestors.com

Bonus Materials

This book comes with bonus materials to help you with your genealogy research in Pennsylvania.

Download your bonuses:
https://www.paancestors.com/book-bonuses

Free introduction to Pennsylvania genealogy course:
https://welcome.paancestors.com

All PA Ancestors books:
https://www.paancestors.com/books/

www.ingramcontent.com/pod-product-compliance
Lightning Source LLC
Chambersburg PA
CBHW070531090426
42735CB00013B/2949